## *Praise for* Winning the Battle for Sales

"It's hard to imagine a more clever way to teach the art and science of selling than *Winning the Battle for Sales*. There's no doubt salespeople will profit from the book's focus on besting one's opponent in a battleground much changed by the information explosion of the Internet, which has provided buyers with an advantage as great as the discovery of gunpowder. But I'd recommend this book for its highly readable retelling of battles and derring-do that changed the world. History lovers will enjoy the modern insights applied to ancient exploits we've often heard of but never really reveled in."

—William Dermody, World/Military Affairs editor, USA Today

"The author does a superb job of looting history for the salient examples of brilliant minds working under extremities of pressure. This book is highly recommended to anyone—from mid- to senior-level manager all the way to young students preparing to enter the exciting field of sales."

—Howard Moon, PhD; military historian; author,
*SST: The Technopolitics of the Tupolev-144*; chief, Islamic
and Regional Issues Staff, Near East Division, CIA, 1992–2004.

"The nineteenth century writer Ambrose Bierce once said that 'War is God's way of teaching Americans geography.' While I doubt John Golden would claim divine inspiration for this text, John has proven that war can successfully teach critical sales techniques. Each battle or incident is carefully chosen to illustrate an important concept in a way that reinforces that concept and better cements it in the mind of the reader than would a straightforward sales training book. As an added bonus, the imagined sounds of thundering hooves and the clash of swords will accompany the aircraft boarding zone announcements on your next sales trip."

—Jay Brinkmann, chief economist and senior vice president
Research and Education, Mortgage Bankers Association

"A good military strategist is after all a salesman, which leads me to believe that a good salesman would make a good military strategist. The author has done an excellent job of showing how those two different communities are in fact very similar ..."

—Brigadier General Julie A Bentz, PhD

"Great sales lessons presented in a really unique and interesting format. I learned some great sales tips and ideas and I picked up a lot of military history along the way. Great, clever approach to help the reader stay engaged and remember the important elements of the book. Great, quick, easy read and I recommend it for sales people starting out in the field as well as seasoned pros."

—Chuck Lennon, president, TeamLogic

"Consider this book proof that John Golden is a member of that exclusive club of *real* sales strategists and he therefore has earned your focused attention. How John ties military victories to successful execution of the B2B sale is clever, educational, and relevant. It's an innovative and very insightful perspective on what it really takes to win."

—Dave Stein, CEO and founder, ES Research Group, Inc.

"I distinctly remember my first VP talking about 'campaigns' and 'targets.' Indeed, successful salespeople have made learning from military tactics an important aspect of their careers. In this engaging read chock full of practical and richly illustrated examples, John Golden provides strategies that are sure to increase even the most seasoned sales pros' success rates. It's a completely new take on sales education with powerful lessons you'll use to win your own sales battles."

—David Meerman Scott, bestselling author
of *The New Rules of Marketing and PR*,
now in over 25 languages from Bulgarian to Vietnamese

# WINNING
## THE
# BATTLE FOR SALES

# WINNING
# THE
# BATTLE FOR SALES

Lessons on Closing Every Deal from
the World's Greatest Military Victories

John Golden

With illustrations by
David M. Connaughton

New York   Chicago   San Francisco   Lisbon   London   Madrid   Mexico City
Milan   New Delhi   San Juan   Seoul   Singapore   Sydney   Toronto

The **McGraw·Hill** Companies

1 2 3 4 5 6 7 8 9 0 DOC/DOC 1 0 9 8 7 6 5 4 3 2

ISBN: 978-0-07-179199-1
MHID: 0-07-179199-X

e-book ISBN: 978-0-07-179200-4
e-book MHID: 0-07-179200-7

McGraw-Hill books are available at special quantity discounts to use as premiums and sales promotions, or for use in corporate training programs. To contact a representative, please e-mail us at bulksales@mcgraw-hill.com.

**Library of Congress Cataloging-in-Publication Data**
Golden, John.
   Winning the battle for sales : lessons on closing every deal from the world's greatest military victories / by John Golden.
      p. cm.
   ISBN-13: 978-0-07-179199-1 (alk. paper)
   ISBN-10: 0-07-179199-X (alk. paper)
   1. Selling. 2. Sales management. 3. Battles—Case studies. 4. Strategy—Case studies.
I. Title.
   HF5438.25.G637 2013
   658.85—dc23

                                                                        2012025254

This book is printed on acid-free paper.

All illustrations used with permission from David M. Connaughton.

*Dedicated to the memory of my father, Thomas Patrick Golden*

# CONTENTS

# INTRODUCTION

Selling is arguably one of the oldest professions. It has been the central core of the human economy from time immemorial. People have been buying and selling goods and services from the beginnings of human interaction. Indeed, writing was likely first invented to record sales of commodities and property, depictions of which represent the oldest writings in Sumerian cuneiform and in Egyptian hieroglyphics—the earliest dating to *ca.* 2600 BC, fairly early in the Bronze Age. Both cuneiform and hieroglyphics had numbers and representations of livestock, birds, grains, and other commodities used in barter—which was the predominant form of trade until the invention of metal money by the Phoenicians *ca.* 1500 BC.

In short, it can be said that selling matters, that it has always mattered. Aside from capital, it is the most important element of wealth creation and sustainment.

History also matters. The great Justice Oliver Wendell Holmes, Jr., said that "a page of history is worth a volume of logic" (*New York Trust Co. v. Eisner*, 256 U.S. 345, 349, 1921). In other words, reality trumps theory. What happens matters more than what *could* happen.

Finally, I contend that military history matters. Often, throughout history, commerce and war are intimately related. But I am not here looking at the relationship between money and combat or trade and hostilities. Rather, in this book I explore military history (because it is fascinating) for lessons that apply to the world of selling (because it matters).

I shall derive lessons from Ancient Egypt to the American West. Because war covers the gamut of human psychology, emotion, and reaction and selling does the same, I shall look to see how the one can inform the other.

There is a tradition as old as the spoken word itself of using anecdotes and events to illustrate points and reinforce concepts. From prophets to politicians (which is quite an expansive gamut!), people have used stories as a way of helping people to understand something and then retain that understanding. In our working lives every day we use the innate skill of *remembering by association* to draw on our rich reservoirs of experience to address challenges and take advantage of opportunities. We have done much, however, through technology to reduce our reliance on good memory function as one of the foundations of our effectiveness. From smart phones and tablets with their exploding array of "apps," to easily accessible online databases of information, to tools that teach and reinforce everything we could possibly ever want to know about how to do our jobs, to "just in time" job aids that help us in our moment of need, it seems that reliance on memory and recall is less important than ever.

So why another sales book, you may ask, particularly one that uses sometimes obscure battles from the furthest outposts of history to illustrate its points? Well, simply put, despite all the new technology-based tools just mentioned, being able to remember and apply good selling skills, strategies, and tactics in an increasingly complex and fast-moving selling environment is becoming more, not less of a challenge. I decided, therefore, to fall back on the tried and tested method of *remembering by association* to introduce (and indeed often reintroduce) some of the fundamental skills, strategies, and tactics of high-performing salespeople and reinforce them through association with military events from history that illustrate the point being made. This is not in any way a glorification of armed conflict—far from it—but as evidenced by the continued robust sales of Sun Tzu's *Art of War*, which was written sometime in the sixth century BC (quotes from which remain a staple of sales presentations the world over), there continues to be that metaphorical association between sales and warfare.

Nevertheless, these are not analogies. In most cases, the "associations" between the battle and the sales lesson are mere wordplay. They are designed simply to help with recall. I do not mean to suggest that there is an analogy between war and selling. War is about zero sum. Selling is about win-win. However, decisions in warfare provide illustrations that can make remembering sales lessons easier. That is my intent. I am simply trying to provide memorable anecdotes and attaching them to lessons for easy recall. Of course, I realize that many of these illustrative tales are a bit of a stretch from the sales perspective—some are amusing, some spot on. But all should be taken with a grain of salt and recognition that this is simply a learning tool, not in any way meant to resemble a comparison.

In 1978, Huthwaite's founder, behavioral psychologist Neil Rackham, began a groundbreaking 12-year research study of sales excellence. It remains to this day the only research effort of its kind. Observing and analyzing more than 35,000 sales calls conducted by the world's leading selling organizations in 27 countries, Neil and his research team were able to isolate and identify distinct behavioral traits of successful sales people.

The results were seminal in that the research pointed to behavioral differentiators as the key to successful selling. These findings gave rise to a number of models and frameworks including SPIN Selling®, Huthwaite's renowned methodology that revolutionized the world of sales and defines consultative selling to this day.

Because the sales lessons I am hoping to pass along are derived from scientifically validated research, they are specific, quantifiable, objective, and observable. They are teachable, repeatable, and measurable. Every year since the completion of the initial study Huthwaite has expanded its research and continually revalidated the validity of the principles through client engagements.

It is my hope that next time you are faced with a selling situation that requires a particular skill or tactic to be successful, you will find a Welsh longbowman, a Roman legionary, or indeed Attila the Hun coming to your aid.

# CHAPTER LAYOUT

Each chapter will—like all Gaul in the time of Julius Caesar—be divided into three parts, symbolized by the following pictures.

## WHAT HAPPENED

Every battle has its winners and losers. History is littered with both glorious and ignominious battles, depending— I suppose—on which side you happened to be rooting for and which side got to write the history. I have tried to look at each encounter from both sides and describe each as impartially as possible.

## WHAT IT MEANT

The battles I have chosen had real significance in their time, and for some, the significance endures. These battles took place all over the world, on land and sea. Some saw the beginnings of empires, some saw the dashed hopes of expanding empires, and some are more akin to pub brawls—but all were massively important to the participants and in some sense important in their time. I shall try to fathom the importance of each.

**SALES LESSON**

What can the aspiring salesperson draw from history's object lessons, lessons on what to do . . . and what not to do? I have drawn lessons from Huthwaite's storied research and relate them to historic encounters. I am of the school that lessons can be learned from history, not only insofar as it ought not be doomed to repeat itself but also as a practical matter across disciplines. I do hope that these anecdotes will help you to remember these perennial truths about sales.

# PART 1
# THE SALES CALL

# 1

## ON PREPARATION

*Forewarned, forearmed; to be prepared is half the victory.*
—MIGUEL DE CERVANTES

General Robert Napier, one of many unrelated Victorian soldiers and sailors named Napier, was a master at preparation. He was sent from Bombay to rescue the British representative and other hostages held by Emperor Tewodros II in Abyssinia. These hostages had been taken because Tewodros was insulted by Queen Victoria's failure to reply to a letter he had sent two years earlier. Napier arrived at Annesley Bay on the East Coast of Africa. The army built piers to help with unloading of the ships and then marched to Tewodros' capital at Magdala. Just before reaching their objective, the army was attacked in force by the Abyssinians but overwhelmingly defeated and repelled them. Napier had taken to heart the lessons learned about the importance of logistics from the Crimean War. His preparation was nearly perfect. Tewodros, after safely releasing the British hostages (and cutting off the hands and feet of the native hostages before tossing them into the precipice), committed suicide.

The sales lesson here is the importance of preparation for sales calls, presentations, and bake-offs. Preparation is distinct from planning in that preparation is homework, background, and understanding the possible problems and opportunities that may come up based on industry knowledge from experience and research. Planning is using that preparation to plan lines of questioning and even specific questions. I shall consider planning in Chapter 2.

**WHAT HAPPENED**

Emperor Tewodros II of Abyssinia, known to the British as Theodore, was a zealous Coptic surrounded by Muslims. He had outlawed the slave trade, suppressed polygamy, manufactured Ethiopia's first cannon, introduced mail, and otherwise sought to restore Ethiopia to its former glory. By 1864, he was on the brink of insanity. A string of personal tragedies, coupled with a susceptibility to instability, had sent him spiraling downward into madness. He had written to Queen Victoria, apparently offering an alliance, and had received no reply. Outraged, he had arrested her consul, Captain Charles Cameron, and his staff, accusing Cameron of plotting with Muslims. He also took about 50 other hostages, including missionaries. It was not his sanest hour.

Three years of failed diplomatic efforts to secure the release of the hostages led to a more martial approach. In 1867, the newly elected Conservative government decided to take a firmer hand. They chose India as a staging area—and more specifically, Bombay, which was just across the Arabian Sea from Abyssinia. The commander of the local army in Bombay was Sir Robert Cornelis Napier, a veteran of both the Indian Mutiny and the Chinese Opium War of 1860. He was an experienced warrior and a sound choice as commander in chief of the relief expedition to Tewodros' mountain fortress at Magdala.

On taking command, he reviewed the situation and decided that the success of the expedition would depend almost wholly on logistics. It would require tremendous preparation. Indeed, the vast majority of the campaign was given over to preparations. Napier concluded that it would require approximately 13,000 fighting men with a host of auxiliaries and camp followers, 8,000 laborers, and 36,000 animals (including horses, asses, camels, and elephants) to accomplish the rescue of the hostages.

His force faced a 420-mile march into the interior of Africa, through hot desert and cold mountains in hostile territory, just to reach the fortress—which was guarded by cannon and widely regarded as impregnable. After freeing the hostages, the army then would have to march back—and all this before the summer rains. It was quite a task, but Napier was the man for it. The base camp was set up at the little fishing village of Zula on Annesley Bay. Napier arrived there on January 2, 1868.

Napier oversaw a series of remarkable engineering feats that aided in transport and secured supply lines through the dangerous terrain that had to be traversed. Sappers and Royal Engineers built a railway from the coast through the desert to the base of the mountains. Then they cleared a wide path through the mountain pass to the 8,000-foot highland plain. Troops and supplies were moved toward the objective with remarkable smoothness and skill.

Further preparations included negotiating safe passage with Ras Kassai through Tigre and Wagshum Gobazi through Lasta (whose wrath was accidentally incurred but as quickly assuaged by monetary compensation). In preparing for the eventual assault, no stone was left unturned. Napier was a brilliant purveyor of assured success. He was no practitioner of the fools rush in approach to military endeavor.

By April 1868, the main force was just about within striking distance of Magdala when the Abyssinians attacked in force. As many as 7,000 warriors armed with muzzleloaders streamed down the hills toward the Arogee plateau. The King's Own and the 27th Beloochee Regiment reached the plateau first and took up position. They numbered about 300 because two companies had been left behind to secure the baggage. It did not look good for the British, except that they had prepared to the hilt. They were armed with the new breech-loading Snider rifle, which could fire a devastating seven rounds a minute. Massively outgunned, the brave Abyssinians were beaten and soon began to retreat. The King's Own steadily pursued until the cautious Napier ordered an end to the counterattack.

It was a quick victory, but the day was not yet won. A large force of Abyssinians, sheltered by a ridge, managed to get around the King's Own and attack what they thought was just the baggage train. Unbeknownst to them, it also included a battery of Royal Artillery and was guarded by a Sikh regiment of Punjab Pioneers. The bearded Sikhs, though themselves armed only with muzzleloaders, were supported by the artillery and eventually set the Abyssinians to flight.

After a grueling night on the field, the British buried 700 bodies—both out of respect for the fallen warriors and for fear of disease. Most of Tewodros' 500 chieftains were among the dead, doubtless because they were mounted and wore scarlet tunics—making them natural targets. Of the 20 British casualties, only two were dead—both Sikhs.

Following the action at Arogee, a frightened and bewildered Tewodros offered to free the hostages but was turned down. Napier possibly feared the reaction of the warlords who had aided him if he were to allow Tewodros his freedom. Napier occupied the now-abandoned heights of Selasse and Fahla and prepared for the final attack.

The assault on Magdala took place on April 13, 1868. It was the work of but a few minutes for the vanguard to scale the walls of the fortress and open the main gate to the victorious British troops. Rather than be taken alive, the emperor apparently shouted, "It is finished!" He then shot himself with a pistol he had received as a gift from Queen Victoria in 1864.

**WHAT IT MEANT**

The success of the Magdala expedition was complete. The hostages were freed, and Tewodros was no more. But more to the point, the success had restored glory to the tarnished reputation of the British Army, which had suffered such humiliation in the Crimea and the Indian Mutiny. It was again an army to be reckoned with. The fame of this little war spread, far out of proportion to its importance in world affairs.

Sir Robert Cornelis Napier returned to England a great hero, having accomplished what many thought was the impossible. He was given the title Baron Napier of Magdala, a hereditary lordship. He died with the rank of field marshal in 1890.

**SALES LESSON**

The lesson from this Victorian adventure centers on the importance of preparation. There is simply no substitute for it. Louis Pasteur once famously said, "Chance favors only the prepared mind." To succeed in sales, as in any science, you must prepare your mind. Indeed, it is the motto of the Boy Scouts: Be prepared. You must know your customers and their business. You must understand their needs, if possible, before they even voice them. To bring value to the marketplace, you must offer insight that actually may take customers by surprise. And to do that, you must prepare yourself. Relentlessly.

First and foremost, do your homework. Do the research. Read analyst reports. Read your customers' press releases, 10K's, 10Q's, and annual reports. Read news stories about your customers. Glean whatever you can about your customers from all the many sources available to you. Supplement your knowledge with social media. Follow your customers on Twitter and Facebook. Learn what you can about individuals in a target account through LinkedIn and other business networks.

Build profiles of your customers that will provide a very solid foundation on which to build value. There is no substitute for hard work—and you'll find it's worth the effort. That's the background.

The next part of preparation for a sales cycle is to organize what you know about the industry of your target account. What do you know from your experience of selling into the industry about business trends affecting your customers and their competitors? What do you know about the problems companies in the particular sector are facing? What do you know about solutions companies are trying? Are some solutions working better than others? Then take the research you have done and weave it into your industry knowledge. How are your customers doing vis-à-vis their competitors? Put together an inventory of what you already know that can potentially be a help to the customers.

Finally, polish up your business acumen. Make sure that you can read a profit and loss (P&L) statement, for example. Great sellers can take a look at a customer's P&L statement and find areas in which they can affect the business beyond just the expense column. Sellers today who do not understand the financials of their customers are unlikely to bring much to the exchange. If they are only affecting the customers' expense columns, they are probably fighting a losing battle. A sale used to be embodied in the exchange of money for a product or service; now it is embodied in the exchange of money for a product or service plus the industry expertise and consultation of the seller. You must understand the five key financial metrics (i.e., revenue, cost of sales, margin, expenses, and profit) and how you can help your customers improve their performance in any of these areas.

The sum of your knowledge from research, personal experience, and business acumen should prepare you adequately to meet customers where they are and provide real value throughout the sales process. However, it is no good just possessing the knowledge, even at your fingertips. You must further prepare for the sales process by organizing all that knowledge into a strategy for how to bring it to bear on behalf of your customers. You are looking to make your customers more successful.

Shortly in this book I shall consider what I call the *value drivers*: helping your customers to discover an unrecognized problem, identify an unanticipated solution, or explore an unseen opportunity—or acting as a broker of capabilities. These are the ways you can profit your customers and reach the coveted position of trusted advisor. To deliver this type of value, you must carefully prepare your mind. You must understand what it is that the customer really needs—even if he or she doesn't yet. You must carefully study the terrain, the topography, and apply all your knowledge to the customer's particular situation. You must think through how you can help the customer to reach the conclusions that will deliver success.

It is a monumental task to prepare properly for the complex sales cycle. But there is no substitute. If you prepare up front—like Napier for Magdala—the engagement may be tremendously foreshortened. The more you prepare, the more likely you are to succeed in the shortest possible time. And once prepared, plan. Plan, plan, plan. But that is the subject for Chapter 2. *Amat victoria curam.*

# 2

## THE NAKED DUEL
## HUMPHREY HOWARTH VERSUS
## THE EARL OF BARRYMORE (1806)

### ON THE IMPORTANCE OF PLANNING

*Whatever failures I have known, whatever errors I have committed,*
*whatever follies I have witnessed in private and public life*
*have been the consequence of action without thought.*
—BERNARD BARUCH

During the racing season at Brighton in 1806, an Irish Peer dueled a nearly naked Member of Parliament after the latter had blackened the former's eye during a game of whist. They met on the racetrack at the appointed hour, and Humphrey Howarth, Member of Parliament, proceeded to strip down to his undershorts—causing great delight among the spectators and some discomfort for Henry Barry, the 8th Earl of Barrymore, who asked what on earth was going on. But Howarth was in earnest. Having earlier in his career worked as a surgeon for the East India Company, he had seen the damage done when a bit of cloth precedes a bullet into a wound. It festers. And often kills by infection.

Howarth had planned, as all salespeople should plan, for all possible outcomes of the meeting. Planning allows for adaptability in the face of adversity. Planning for contingencies equips you with multiple paths to get to your destination. General Eisenhower did say that plans are nothing; planning is everything.

**WHAT HAPPENED**

Back in 1806, in Brighton, England, an Irish aristocrat, Henry Barry, 8th Earl of Barrymore, and a politician, Humphrey Howarth, Member of Parliament for Evesham, were engaged in a game of whist (a forerunner of the card game bridge) at the rather raucous Castle Inn. It being racing season in the town, there was, as you can imagine, much merrymaking (a forerunner of partying) going on. Probably the most lethal cocktail at the inn that evening was the combination of alcohol, competitive card playing, entitled nobility, and opinionated legislator. Almost inevitably an argument broke out when the aristocrat called the politician "false" over a particular card, at which point the parliamentarian dispensed with the usual verbal tools of his trade and instead elected to administer a right hook, leaving the Earl with a black eye and an even blacker mood. The Earl immediately issued a challenge to a duel, and despite it already being one in the morning, the two men agreed to meet on the field of honor at 5 a.m. (honor in those days was not something to be kept waiting).

At the appointed time, they both appeared on the said field of honor, which happened to be the racetrack, in keeping with the whole sporting/gambling nature of the chain of events that had led them to this point. Before the pistols were even in the hands of the combatants, the eccentric parliamentarian, despite the early morning chill, began to remove his clothing until he stood there in nothing but his drawers. By this time, a large crowd had gathered and people were laughing hysterically at the sight of the elderly, rather rotund, and near-naked politician who was now standing, pistol in hand, nonchalantly waiting for the duel to begin. Both the seconds, Sir John Shelley for Howarth and Mr. Mellish for the Earl, were rather amused.

Now Howarth was well known as somewhat of a mischief maker—as indeed was his adversary, the Earl, who asked him to please explain what he meant by this foolishness. To his surprise, the politician was not doing it for shock value or for the amusement of the crowd but rather for a very practical reason. It turned out that when he was much younger, he had been a surgeon with the British East India Company. There he had seen what often resulted when a man was shot and the bullet forced some of his clothing deep into the wound. In many cases, it was relatively straightforward to extract the bullet but very difficult to remove the cloth that had now become embedded in the wound. The wound then would get infected, often resulting in the death of the individual. Howarth therefore figured that if the duel did not go his way and he had the misfortune to be wounded, his chances of living to fight another day were greatly increased if the bullet entered his body cleanly and could be removed quickly without the complication of embedded clothing.

His unorthodox approach actually paid off, not because he was wounded and the lack of clothing saved him but rather because the Earl decided that it was ridiculous to fight a naked man. They both fired into the air, and honor was deemed satisfied.

**WHAT IT MEANT**

The "Nude Duel" is little more than a curiosity in the historical annals of dueling. It had no great impact on dueling, history generally—or even on the moment. People snickered as word got around, but the duel did not affect Howarth's career more than to somewhat solidify his reputation as an eccentric, nor did it affect the reputation of Barry, who had been dubbed "Cripplegate" by the Prince of Wales owing to his having a clubfoot. Henry Barry was almost as dissolute as his elder brother and best friend Richard, the 7th Earl of Barrymore. Richard also was an intimate of the future King George IV and was called "Hellgate" for reasons not hard to imagine. He died young in a bizarre gun accident and passed his tarnished title to Henry. The third brother, Augustus Barry, earned the sobriquet "Newgate" owing apparently to the fact that he had been imprisoned in every jail in England—except Newgate, the prison for women. It just goes to show: Watergate, Irangate, Monicagate—there is no new scandal under the sun.

**SALES LESSON**

Planning calls is one of the most effective and most neglected activities in sales. There is simply no substitute for good planning, and yet it is rarely done. If the eccentric old Member of Parliament has anything to teach us, it is this: Plan, plan, plan. For all possible outcomes.

It's probably safe to say that most salespeople don't spend enough time planning and that the effort they do put into planning is often misdirected.

There are three types of sales plans: account, opportunity, and call. The temptation is to concentrate on strategic account planning—the high-level game plan. However, the planning that sellers usually neglect is at the level of the sales call.

As budgets for travel shrink, every meeting becomes that much more vitally important; every face-to-face engagement matters that much more. For many, the short period of intense anxiety in the elevator on the way up to a customer meeting serves as a substitute for planning. It shouldn't. *Gladiator in arena consilium capit.*

Call planning done properly should take a little time and effort. It should adequately prepare the salesperson to maximize every moment of time in the presence of the customer. Done properly, it will pay off in spades. Let's take a look at what the good call plan includes.

The first thing that ought to be defined is the desired outcome of the call. First, let's note that there are four possible outcomes of any sales call. These are

1. *No sale*—This is self-evident. It is where the salesperson is shut down with a definitive, "No, we will not do business with you." The sales cycle will not continue.
2. *Continuation*—In this case, the sale has not been terminated, but neither has it been moved forward. The customer may have liked the presentation or the demonstration, maybe even a lot, but has made no commitment that progresses the sale.
3. *Advance*—This is a commitment or action by the customer that actually moves the sale forward toward a successful conclusion.
4. *Order*—The ultimate goal of the sales process, this is where the customer signs on the dotted line.

To be considered successful, a sales call should result in an advance or an order. In complex sales, an order is not the primary objective of most sales calls. This is not because an order is undesirable. On the contrary, an order would be great any time. This is so because in most sales calls in a complex sales cycle an order is simply an unrealistic goal—until the time comes.

In a sales cycle that demands multiple calls, one should always be planning for the advance: that is, an action, either in the call or after it, that moves the sale forward toward a decision. And that action should be on the part of the customer. And a planned advance should meet the SMART criteria; that is, it should be *s*pecific, *m*easurable, *a*ction-oriented, *r*ealistic, and *t*ime-based. Some examples of advances might include the customer providing access to a decision maker who was previously off-limits, or the customer agreeing to come and see a demonstration off-site, or the customer agreeing to test your product for a trial period. Anything that actually keeps up the momentum of the sale can be considered an advance. Plan for advances.

Without a planned advance, a sales call is highly likely to result in a continuation. Salespeople unfortunately are often delighted with a continuation because they don't know the difference. A continuation may sound positive and upbeat—"Loved the presentation!" or "Nice demonstration—we were all very impressed!" These are nice words to hear, but they do not practically move the sale forward. They require no action or commitment on the part of the customer. Define the advance that would move the sale forward in each call, and plan to achieve that advance.

How does one determine what the advance should be? It is wise to aim for the largest realistic increment of commitment from the customer. Game-winning drives are usually assembled from a series of shorter gains. Having chosen the desirable advance, the next thing is to establish both a less ambitious advance—a fallback position—and a more ambitious advance. It is important to be prepared for whatever happens in the meeting.

Next, the salesperson should think through and write down an assessment of the current situation that the customer is facing. What are the business issues, challenges, and marketplace trends that are affecting the customer? Then move from the general to the specific: What are the customer's actual needs? Have they been expressed, and do they need to be developed? Are they *implied* needs (admitted but with no urgency to act) or *explicit* needs (spoken with an affirmation of intent to act)?

Once you've worked out a best guess at the customer's probable needs, it's time to begin exploring the call itself. What SPIN questions will you ask to guide the discussion to a successful outcome? Is there any information that you absolutely need to know? Plan the *situation* questions that will elicit the answers you need. Then write down a few *problem* questions that will get the customer thinking down the track you are headed. What are the *implications* of these problems? What do you need to ask to build the urgency to solve the problem? And finally, prepare a few *need-payoff* questions—questions that will get the customer to say out loud how your solution will solve the problem.

When you have a general outline of your proposed discussion, with questions that will direct it where you want it to go, make one final preparation: Plan how you will open with a customer-centered purpose based on your planned outcome. If you plan your calls thus, you will be thoroughly prepared to use your precious time with the customer as wisely as possible. Neglect planning, and you will waste your own time. Worse, you will waste your customer's time. And that is unforgivable.

# 3

## OPENING THE CALL

*Quite unique among chess openings, the King's gambit is especially apt for talent, for genius, for heroism.*
—TONY SANTASIERE

Trafalgar was one of the great naval battles in history. The British Royal Navy spectacularly defeated the combined French and Spanish navies during the Napoleonic Wars. The outcome established British naval superiority for the next hundred years. Employing brilliant tactics, Admiral Nelson was able to destroy the Franco-Spanish fleet (22 of 33 ships of the line) without the loss of a single British ship (of 27 ships of the line). His opening gambit was perhaps the most critical part of the battle. *E mare libertas.*

The takeaway from a sales perspective has to do with the relative importance of opening the call and the skills necessary to do it most effectively.

The Battle of Trafalgar was extraordinary in that it arrayed the British Royal Navy against the combined French and Spanish fleets in the first pitched naval battle in the 16 years they had been at constant war. Vice Admiral Viscount Lord Nelson was a man to be reckoned with. Literally. Admiral Villeneuve was holed up in the Spanish harbor at Cadiz, turning a deaf ear to the Napoleonic rage that sought his ships in the English Channel for invasion transport. Villeneuve was just plain afraid of Nelson. Apparently more so than of the little Corsican. Until at last he received (false) intelligence from an American captain that Nelson was still in London, at which time he at last heeded Napoleon's stinging rebukes and ventured out to run the blockade of small British frigates. He was, of course, unaware that the main Royal Navy commanded by Nelson himself was awaiting him at sea.

When it was too late for Villeneuve to turn and flee, Nelson and His Majesty's Ship *Victory* appeared over the horizon. Villeneuve and Admirals d'Aliva and Cisternas of Spain prepared for battle in the traditional arc arrangement of ships of the line.

Nelson, by contrast, took a most unorthodox approach to the enemy line. Rather than preparing his force in an opposing parallel line for orthodox broadside battle, Nelson divided his numerically inferior fleet into two squadrons that attacked perpendicularly. Such was his most unusual and most effective opening of the great battle. The flagship

*Victory* attacked a third of the way down the enemy line, cutting the center and vanguard off from the rest of the combined fleet. The light wind took the vanguard out of the fight almost completely because it took a long time to turn around and sail back into the fray. They arrived too late to help. Meanwhile, Vice Admiral Collingwood in HMS *Royal Sovereign* attacked two-thirds of the way down the line, cutting off the rear.

Nelson sailed fully rigged for a point between the French flagship *Bucentaure* and the French *Redoubtable*. They were too close together, so *Victory* simply rammed *Redoubtable* and fired broadsides at both ships as it scraped between them. The ships following *Victory* engaged the French and Spanish ships as they came up. Such was Nelson's unorthodox strategy.

As for the difference in tactics between the two fleets, the French and Spanish aimed their broadsides at enemy decks and masts with a view to disabling and destroying the ships' maneuverability. The Royal Navy, by contrast, aimed their broadsides below decks into the enemy cannons, disabling guns and gun crews and creating general mayhem. British casualties were 1,587. And although French and Spanish casualties have never been revealed, they are generally estimated to be approximately 16,000. British gunners were more skilled.

Admiral Viscount Lord Nelson, in full dress regalia on the deck of the *Victory*, was hit by a musket ball from a sharpshooter in the rigging of the *Redoubtable*. He was taken to the cockpit, where he died an hour later after being assured of the glorious British victory.

**WHAT IT MEANT**

The Battle of Trafalgar ushered in the Pax Britannica, England's unchallenged control of the world's major maritime trade routes and sea power generally for more than a century. It also forced Napoleon to give up his dreams of invading the British Isles. In the days following Trafalgar, confined to the European continent, Napoleon broke up his invasion force at Boulogne and marched his troops to Austria, where he crushed the combined Austrian and Russian forces at Austerlitz (cold comfort!) and continued his dominance—offering, incidentally, another sales lesson regarding untended markets!

**SALES LESSON**

Opening the call effectively matters. But it doesn't matter nearly as much as one might suppose. In fact, Huthwaite's research into call preliminaries reveals some surprising insights.

For example, first impressions, unless for some reason notably disastrous, don't make or break a call. There's evidence to suggest that people notice far less in the early stages of an interaction than we may imagine. Nondescript or even awkward openings can be easily overcome and lead to successful outcomes. In the early stages of an interaction with another person, we're usually so overloaded with information that we either don't notice or we quickly forget some quite obvious things. How often have you been introduced to someone and 10 seconds later forgotten his or her name? Why should you forget something as important as a name? Because your mind is full of other things, such as what you're going to say next. You literally don't have room for all the details available to you. Many potentially important impressions get crowded out in the opening minutes of a meeting.

Traditionally, salespeople have been taught that not only does the opening matter, but it is in fact crucial. According to the conventional wisdom, there are two successful ways to open a call:

- *Relate to the buyer's personal interests.* This has to do with developing a relationship quickly. The reasoning is that if you can meet the buyer on some personal level, it will smooth things. For example, if there is a prominently displayed photograph of the buyer's prize fish on the desk, talk fishing. If there's a photo of what appear to be his or her children on the desk, talk family. This is, of course, nonsense and can easily backfire. Hold off on getting personal with customers. Relationships develop with time and mutual interests—and while they matter on a personal level, they don't guarantee brand loyalty anyway.
- *Make an opening benefit statement.* The logic goes that you can wow a customer by opening with a dramatic statement of how your product or service can benefit him or her. In fact, this doesn't make much difference to the customer—and on the down side, it

may trap you into discussing your product or service too early. In addition, salespeople who always open their calls with a benefit statement tend to sound scripted—which has no positive impact. It is probably best to leave the conventional wisdom in the case of call openings on the table.

There isn't one best opening technique. But there is a framework that successful people use. What is the objective of your opening? At its very simplest, what you're trying to do is to get the customer's consent to move on to the next phase—the investigating stage. You want customers to agree that it's legitimate for you to ask them some questions. In order to do this, you must establish

- Who you are
- Why you're there (but not by giving product details)
- Your right to ask questions

Obviously, there are many ways to open the call, but the common factor of most good openings is that they lead the customer to agree that you should ask the questions. In doing so, good openings keep you from getting into detailed discussions of products or services. Early in the call you want to establish your role as the seeker of information and the buyer's role as the giver.

Preliminaries, as I've said, don't play a crucial role. The most important test of whether you're handling the preliminaries effectively is whether your customers are generally happy to move ahead and answer your questions. If so, then you're probably handling this stage of the call acceptably. Don't worry about appearing smooth and polished. Worry about this:

1. *Get down to business quickly.* Don't dawdle. The preliminaries stage is not the most productive part of the call for you or for the customer. A common mistake is spending too long on pleasantries. As a result, the call runs short of time—the customer has to stop just when you're getting to a critical point. Don't feel that

you'll offend customers by getting down to business quickly. A complaint I frequently hear from senior executives and professional buyers is that salespeople waste their time with idle chatter. I've never heard the complaint that a salesperson gets down to business too quickly.

2. *Don't talk about solutions too soon.* One of the most common mistakes in selling is talking about your solutions and capabilities too early in the call. Offering solutions too soon causes objections and greatly reduces the chances that the call will succeed. How often do you find yourself discussing your products, services, or solutions with the customer during the first half of the call? If it happens frequently, then it may be a sign that you're not handling the preliminaries effectively. If it's usually the customer who is asking the questions and you're in the role of providing facts and explanations, then it's likely that you've not sufficiently established your role as a questioner during the preliminaries. Ask yourself whether your call opening establishes that you should be asking the questions. If it doesn't establish this, then change the way you open calls so that the customer accepts that you'll be asking some questions before you talk about the capabilities you can offer.

3. *Concentrate on questions.* Never forget that preliminaries aren't the most important part of the call. Too often salespeople waste time before a call worrying about how they should open it when they should be using that time far more effectively to plan some questions instead.

Admiral Nelson opened the Battle of Trafalgar with a brilliant and stunning gambit. The cunning genius of the perpendicular attack quite possibly assured his success from the outset. The same can rarely be said for the opening of a sales call. The great thing is to keep your priorities straight and move on from the preliminaries with some vim.

# 4

## ON NOT PRESENTING TOO EARLY:
## THE SPIN MODEL

*He that will have a cake out of the wheat must tarry the grinding.*
—WILLIAM SHAKESPEARE

In 217 BC, Fabius Maximus was given the honor of defending Rome against Hannibal's vastly superior Carthaginian invasion force. Aware of his army's inferior military prowess, Fabius employed a policy of harassment and delay rather than allowing a pitched battle—which he would surely lose. He stayed near to Hannibal's army, just out of reach, exercising a scorched-earth policy to prevent Hannibal from feeding his troops. It was a strategy of slow attrition.

The lesson for salespeople is that it is a wise policy to await the appropriate time to present your offerings. You must first, as it were, build the pain through bringing problems and their implications to light by asking incisive and insightful questions.

**WHAT HAPPENED**

Quintus Fabius Maximus, an eminent Roman Consul and general, had the sobriquet "Cunctator"—"the Delayer"— for his strategy for handling Hannibal's invasion of Italy in the Second Punic War. He was also nicknamed "Verrucosus," or "warty"—for a wart above his upper lip. But that is neither here nor there.

Fabius Maximus was appointed dictator in 217 BC following the death of C. Flaminius in battle. Fabius's policy was beautifully summed up by Plutarch: "Fabius . . . thought it not seasonable to engage with the enemy. . . . [I]n regard that the Carthaginians were but few, and in want of money and supplies, he deemed it best not to meet in the field a general whose army had been tried in many encounters, and whose object was a battle, but to send aid to their allies, control the movements of the various subject cities, and let the force and vigor of Hannibal waste away and expire, like a flame, for want of aliment" (Plutarch, *Lives of Illustrious Men*, "Fabius").

Alive to Carthaginian military superiority, Fabius refused to meet Hannibal on the open field. Instead, he kept his army in the hills above the Carthaginian army and followed them everywhere, staying on the high ground and continually harassing foraging parties. In addition, his scorched-earth policy prevented Hannibal's army from collecting sustenance from the countryside. Hannibal was desperate to fight.

"But this his dilatory way gave occasion in his own camp for suspicion of want of courage; and this opinion prevailed yet more in Hannibal's army. Hannibal was himself the only man who was not deceived, who discerned his skill and detected his tactics, and saw, unless he could by art or force bring him to battle, that the Carthaginians, unable to use the arms in which they were superior, and suffering the continual drain of lives and treasure in which they were inferior, would in the end come to nothing" (Plutarch, *Lives of Illustrious Men*, "Fabius").

It does have to be said that Fabius's approach was not universally applauded by the Romans. Many considered him a coward. Twice the Romans tried their hand at fighting Hannibal in the field. Twice they were slaughtered.

The first time, Minucius Rufus (Fabius's master of the horse) openly defied Fabius by attacking a few columns of Carthaginians, who retreated. Although it was a meaningless victory, it spurred Minucius to greater ambition, and using political connections in Rome, he got himself essentially chosen co-dictator. Fabius gave him half the army but sternly warned him not to attack Hannibal. Once again, Minucius was overcome by his natural desire to crush the invaders and so engaged Hannibal at Larinum. His army would have been utterly destroyed had not Fabius raced in and sent the Carthaginians packing.

The second time the Fabian strategy (as it is now known) was ignored was after Fabius's term as dictator was up. Caius Terentius Varro, who was most eager to engage the invaders, had been elected Consul with Lucius Aemilius Paullus. Varro was spoiling for a fight. The result was the Battle of Cannae in 216 BC. Hannibal utterly trounced the Romans. The defeat sent shock waves throughout Italy. At last, even his political enemies realized that Fabius had been right all along. In 215 BC, Fabius was elected Consul, and he quickly reverted to his tried and true delaying and harassing tactics. He was now held in high honor, and his doctrine was universally appreciated by the Romans.

In the end, Hannibal's invasion did indeed come to nothing. The war of attrition waged by Fabius Maximus had been successful. Fabius opposed the expedition of Scipio Africanus to Carthage in 205 BC to

finish the job. He died before the final crushing and decisive victory of
the Romans over Hannibal's army at the Battle of Zama in 202 BC. So
ended the Second Punic War.

**WHAT IT MEANT**

Fabius has given his name to the military strategy of waiting, which was employed to great advantage by General
George Washington in the American Revolution: Fabian—
using delaying tactics and avoiding direct confrontation.

The term also was famously adopted by the early
British socialist movement as a political strategy in the
middle of the nineteenth century. The Fabian Society, as it was called,
promoted a kind of "wait until the people are enlightened" rather than
a "throw the bums out" approach to the spread of socialist ideals. The
latter approach was chosen by Karl Marx and Friedrich Engels, who literally wrote the book on revolution (*The Communist Manifesto*). Lenin
followed the Marxist credo ("Workers of the world, unite!") and might
have added, "And destroy!"—but didn't. Few now would dispute that
the British Labour Party is a more appropriate political apparatus than,
for example, the Union of Soviet Socialist Republics. Anyway, it is certainly a more peaceful solution. The Fabian Society is still operating
as a left-of-center think tank for the Labour Party, which it is largely
responsible for having created.

Having said that, while waiting may be a generally more palatable
political option than revolt, there does come a time for action in warfare—as there does in sales. Scipio Africanus had to finish the war with
a decisive blow. Salespeople likewise do have to demonstrate capability.

**SALES LESSON**

Fabius held back on fighting a pitched battle for startlingly
good reasons, as we have seen. And his ploy met with huge
success at the end of the day. But why should salespeople
hold back on anything . . . ever? What should a salesperson
be waiting for?

One of the biggest traps inexperienced sellers fall
into is introducing their solution too early. This is so tempting and so
common that I frequently caution against it. Successful sellers don't

talk about their products, services, or the benefit of their solution until they have carefully engineered the right circumstances. In other words, sellers should practice a Fabian policy regarding what has been called the "show up and throw up" approach to sales.

Here's why.

A *need* is any statement made by a buyer that expresses a concern or a desire. In Huthwaite, buyers have two kinds of needs: implied needs and explicit needs. *Implied needs* are needs expressed as problems, difficulties, or dissatisfaction:

"I'm concerned about . . ."
"We are not happy with . . ."

*Explicit needs* are needs that are clear statements of strong wants or desires.

"We must have a solution to . . ."
"What I want is . . ."

The fundamental job of a salesperson early in the sales cycle with a potential customer is to generate an explicit need for his or her product or service. This is done first by uncovering pent-up needs by asking questions about problems and dissatisfaction. These are usually expressed as implied needs initially. Then, by further questioning, develop and expand those needs in the mind of the customer until he or she is overcome by a pressing desire to take action. Of course, that is the ideal. This usually will take more than one call in a complex sale. Sometimes many, many calls. But the idea is to move the customer from complacency to urgency by asking pointed questions—and then listening carefully to the answers.

This might be a good time to give a quick overview of the SPIN model because it happens to be an outstanding model for developing implied into explicit needs. *SPIN* is an acronym for Situation Questions, Problem Questions, Implication Questions, and Need-Payoff Questions. These questions represent the sequence of questions that typically is followed by an excellent salesperson. The sequence is not chiseled in stone and is not even really the point. It is the types of questions and how well they are used that matter. And, of course, the answers matter most.

- *Situation Questions* are questions regarding facts and background information. They are necessary, particularly early in the sales cycle, but they should be used sparingly because they tend to bore the customer.
- *Problem Questions* are questions about, not surprisingly, problems, difficulties, or dissatisfaction with the status quo. They are used to uncover implied needs and to give the salesperson a broad sense of the lay of the land.
- *Implication Questions* are questions about the effects or consequences of the problems expressed. They are used to take a problem that the buyer perceives to be relatively unimportant and build it up into a problem large enough to justify action; in other words, they are used to develop implied into explicit needs.
- *Need-Payoff Questions* are questions about the value or usefulness of the solution. They are used to get the customer to focus on the solution rather than the problem (which may be depressing and therefore may be psychologically unfavorable for the seller). And the seller gets the customer to voice the benefits of the seller's solution. This is important because humans value more what they say themselves than what they are told.

The importance of an explicit need on the table cannot be overstated. Implied needs are not powerful buying signals. Explicit needs, on the other hand, are strongly related to sales success. When a buyer states an explicit need, it is time for the salesperson to move the sale forward; it is time to demonstrate capability. It is the moment, as they say, for action.

Since the 1920s, sellers have been taught that there are two ways to demonstrate capability. One is by using *features*; the other is by using *benefits*. Features are facts about a product or service and are unpersuasive (the buyer would do better just to read the brochure than waste his or her time with a salesperson who merely cites interesting information about a product's accessories). Benefits show how the features can help the customer and are traditionally held in high esteem. As it turns out, there are two types of benefit that crop up in effective sales. One is the traditional view: A benefit shows how a product or service can be used or can help the customer. The other shows how a product or service meets an explicit need expressed by the customer.

To make the distinction, Huthwaite has chosen to call the first type an *advantage* and the second type a *benefit*. The difference is slight, but it is ever so important in effective sales. Advantages do have a slightly positive impact on buyers, but benefits are extremely powerful. Connecting your solution to an expressed explicit need has a tremendous impact on the buyer.

And so the Fabian stratagem proves effective in sales. Fabius waited (and waited) until the opposing army defeated itself by attrition. Salespeople need to wait until they hear the explicit need before they leap in with a solution. A solution presented when the buyer's need is small has little impact. If the seller can develop a strong need, then the solution will have much increased impact on the buyer. The great thing is to get all the needs on the table, develop them into actionable problems, and then—and only then, when an explicit need is on the table—should you present your offering. Presenting too early is the death knell to many an otherwise hopeful sale. Learn to wait. *Unus homo nobis cunctando restituit rem.*

# 5

## THE VALUE DRIVERS:
## THE UNRECOGNIZED PROBLEM

*A lot of people in our industry haven't had very diverse experiences.*
*So they don't have enough dots to connect, and they end up with very linear*
*solutions without a broad perspective on the problem.*
— STEVE JOBS

In 1789, 18 sailors on a British ship sent to gather Tahitian bread-fruit for Jamaican slaves mutinied and took over His Majesty's Ship (HMS) *Bounty* or, more precisely, His Majesty's Armed Vessel (HMAV) *Bounty*. The mutineers, led by Master's Mate Fletcher Christian, sailed back to Tahiti and picked up several locals. They then sailed to the desolate Pitcairn Island and scuttled the ship. Captain Bligh sailed a 23-foot skiff 4,000 miles to safety in Timor. He never did understand his mutinous crew, which just goes to show that you need to help your customers understand the unrecognized problem.

The lesson for salespeople is on the importance of the *unrecognized problem* as a driver of value in the complex sale.

**WHAT HAPPENED**

HMS *Bounty* was moored in the beautiful waters of Tahiti for nearly six months during the warm season (as distinct from the other slightly less warm season) of 1788–1789. During those lovely, lazy months in paradise, crew members collected and propagated breadfruit seedlings under the watchful eye of botanist David Nelson, nursing 1,015 of them to a certain robustness for the long journey to Jamaica. Also during that idyllic spring and summer south of the equator, crew members collected stunning Tahitian mistresses.

Needless to say, many crew members were displeased and to a degree uncooperative when it came time to shove off. Romantic bliss gave way to hard sailing. By the time they were a month out to sea, crew members were downright rebellious.

Murmuring gave way to action. On April 4, 1789, Master's Mate Fletcher Christian led a mutiny against a genuinely nonplussed Captain William Bligh, who couldn't seem to fathom the psychology of the mutineers. He simply did not recognize the problem. *Concordia salus.*

In fact, Bligh had treated Fletcher Christian to a fair amount of public humiliation. On land, this no doubt would have resulted in a duel between the two. But dueling at sea was strictly forbidden by the Royal Navy. Of course, so was mutiny. But, for Christian, who claimed anyway to have been in hell already, the unthinkable became thinkable.

According to Captain Bligh's account [*William Bligh's Narrative of the Mutiny on the Bounty and the Voyage of the Ship's Launch* (London: George Nicol, 1790) A Narrative, &c.]:

Just before sun-rising, Mr. Christian, with the master at arms, gunner's mate, and Thomas Burket, seaman, came into my cabin while I was asleep, and seizing me, tied my hands with a cord behind my back, and threatened me with instant death, if I spoke or made the least noise: I, however, called so loud as to alarm everyone; but they had already secured the officers who were not of their party, by placing centinels [*sic*] at their doors. There were three men at my cabin door, besides the four within; Christian had only a cutlass in his hand, the others had muskets and bayonets. I was hauled out of bed, and forced on deck in my shirt, suffering great pain from the tightness with which they had tied my hands. I demanded the reason of such violence, but received no other answer than threats of instant death, if I did not hold my tongue. Mr. Elphinston, the master's mate, was kept in his birth [*sic*]; Mr. Nelson, botanist, Mr. Peckover, gunner, Mr. Ledward, surgeon, and the master, were confined to their cabins; and also the clerk, Mr. Samuel, but he soon obtained leave to come on deck. The fore hatchway was guarded by centinels [*sic*]; the boatswain and carpenter were, however, allowed to come on deck, where they saw me standing abaft the mizen-mast, with my hands tied behind my back, under a guard, with Christian at their head.

Christian was not to be deterred from the path he had chosen. The die was cast. The ship was taken without bloodshed or any more of a struggle than Bligh himself put up.

Bligh was lowered into a 23-foot open launch with 18 officers and loyalist crew members. After much abuse, a great deal of ridicule, and some sport, they were unceremoniously cast adrift. Provisions on the small boat, according to Captain Bligh, included twine, canvas, lines, sails, cordage, a 28-gallon cask of water, and 150 pounds of bread with a small quantity of rum and wine, as well as a quadrant and compass. Mr. Samuel, Bligh's clerk, was forbidden on pain of death to touch the map, ephemeris, book of astronomical observations, sextant, time keeper, or any of Captain Bligh's surveys or drawings. At the last minute, the castaways were thrown four cutlasses. That's it.

Captain Bligh's adventure had just begun. He led his outcast crew on an epic, eventful, and grueling voyage of almost 4,000 miles, landing safely in Timor in the Dutch East Indies 41 days later. He returned to England, reported the mutiny to the Admiralty, and two years later commanded a second breadfruit expedition to the South Pacific in the *Providence* and the *Assistant*. This 1791 voyage was more successful, resulting in a Royal Society medal for Captain Bligh.

Christian Fletcher and the 25 remaining crew members, not all of whom had taken part in the mutiny but were the most able of the ship's company, returned to Tahiti and made off with 6 Polynesian men and 12 women—quite possibly against their collective will. They sailed to a desolate Pitcairn Island and settled the place. The mutineers then burned the *Bounty*, certainly to prevent detection and possibly to prevent desertion. They tried to set up a utopian society, which failed. And they lived ever after. At least until they had killed each other off. Interestingly, there are to this day descendants of the mutineers on Pitcairn Island (which is still desolate).

**WHAT IT MEANT**

The mutiny on the *Bounty* has captured the popular imagination ever since. Its fame was secured by the publishing of Sir John Barrow's, *The Eventful History of the Mutiny and Piratical Seizure of HMS Bounty: It's Causes and Consequences*, in 1831. Since then, literally dozens of books have been written, screenplays have been filmed, and plays have been performed depicting the adventures of Captain Bligh, Fletcher Christian, and the mutineers. Fletcher Christian has been portrayed on the big screen by no less than Errol Flynn (*In the Wake of the Bounty*, 1933), Clark Gable (*Mutiny on the Bounty*, 1935), Marlon Brando (*Mutiny on the Bounty*, 1962) and Mel Gibson (*The Bounty*, 1984).

With a population of only around 50, the people of Pitcairn are descended from the mutineers of HMS *Bounty* and their Tahitian companions. Pitcairn Island is approximately 2 miles long and 1 mile wide with the capital, Adamstown, located above Bounty Bay and accessed by the aptly named road, The Hill of Difficulty.

The *Bounty's* original mission was to provide a new and cheap crop to feed the British slaves of the West Indies. Breadfruit seemed the perfect solution, although the slaves ultimately rejected it on the grounds that it was inedible. It is now a staple food source throughout the Caribbean.

The lesson we draw from the mutiny on the *Bounty* has to do with helping the customer to discover the unrecognized problem. It is the first of four value drivers that will help salespeople to escape the price-driven sale.

Huthwaite research shows that customers are willing to pay a premium, redefine the buyer-seller relationship, erect barriers to the seller's competitors, and establish the seller as a trusted advisor when

1. The seller reveals to the buyer an *unrecognized problem* that the buyer or the buyer's organization is experiencing.
2. The seller establishes for the buyer an *unanticipated solution* to the problems that the buyer or the buyer's organization is experiencing.
3. The seller creates or reveals an *unseen opportunity* for the buyer or the buyer's organization.
4. The seller serves as more than just a vendor of products or services but instead serves as a *broker of capabilities*. Specifically, the seller serves to make available to the buyer the full range of capabilities of the seller's organization in such a way that these capabilities contribute to an expansion or redefinition of the customer's success.

Bligh had a problem, but he did not recognize it as such. And it was his downfall on the *Bounty*. The salesperson who can help the customer to discover an unrecognized problem will be amply rewarded. I describe the unrecognized problem as any difficulty that needs to be resolved but is unknown. That is, the customer's business is suffering from some malady that he or she is not aware of—the customer's bottom line is being adversely affected by a hidden cause.

That said, let's look at the unrecognized problem as a tool of the clever salesperson to be used on behalf of the customer. How can the salesperson possibly recognize a problem that the customer himself or herself doesn't even see. It is a matter of the convergence of two things that the salesperson brings to the table in a way that the customer doesn't.

The first is *business acumen*. The customer may understand the ins and outs of his or her business better than anyone else. In fact, of course, he or she does. But the salesperson has a very deep and particular understanding of the business issues that his or her own product or service can effect. The salesperson has experience dealing with profit and loss (P&L) statements in a wide variety of businesses and industries. He or she has seen things the customer has never seen.

The second is *industry knowledge*. Again, the customer hopefully understands his or her industry with extreme thoroughness. But what he or she doesn't have—and can't really have—is the experience of his or her competitors. The salesperson, by contrast, can and does have experience across the industry. He or she has seen the problems that his or her customer's competitors are facing. The salesperson understands and has helped them solve those problems with his or her products and services. And the salesperson can extrapolate. He or she can imagine that perhaps his or her customer is experiencing the same things, even if the customer doesn't see them.

The job of the salesperson who hopes to bring extra value to customers by helping them to discover the unrecognized problem is this: Find at the convergence of his or her industry knowledge and business acumen the needs that customers are likely to have and the problems that they are probably experiencing unawares and show them to them. The job of the salesperson is to illuminate the problems through careful questioning.

I say through careful questioning because it is rather important that customers reach their own conclusions regarding the existence of the problem. This is so because of what I call the *boundary conditions* of communication, which arise from what is known in behavioral psychology as the *confirmation bias*:

1. People value what *they say* and their own conclusions more than what *they are told.*
2. People value what *they ask for* more than what is *freely offered.*

In other words, no one likes to have answers shoved down their throat. Even if the answers are correct—sometimes especially if they are correct. Unsolicited advice comes across as criticism. And most people don't like to be criticized. Thus the importance of outstanding questioning skills, as manifested by the SPIN model. Asking questions does not make one a consultative seller. It is asking the right questions at the right time that matters. If a question can produce a Eureka! moment in the mind of the customer or elicit an invitation to speak freely, then it has done its job.

Thus, actually, the unrecognized problem is delivered at the convergence of three things: business acumen, industry knowledge, and questioning skill. We shall look at these in more detail in the next few chapters. The important thing to understand is that the salesperson will uncover unrecognized problems—and thereby deliver tremendous value—by studying what he or she already knows, memorializing it, and then drawing the customer out. It is a matter of preparation. It is a matter of figuring out from experience what problems the customer may be experiencing that he or she might not be aware of.

Bligh no doubt would have been grateful if someone had made clear the depths of the unhappiness on the ship by questioning him carefully about the situation. It might have been very different if the unrecognized problem had been brought properly to his attention.

# 6

## THE VALUE DRIVERS:
## THE UNANTICIPATED SOLUTION

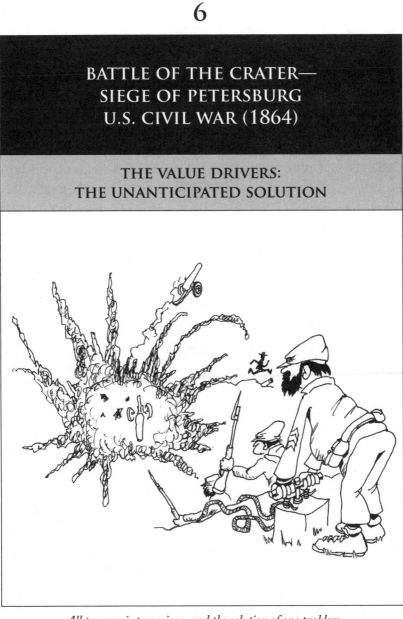

*All progress is precarious, and the solution of one problem
brings us face to face with another problem.*
— MARTIN LUTHER KING, JR.

In the summer of 1864, during the Siege of Petersburg, the U.S. Army conceived the idea of literally blowing a hole in the Confederate defenses. They dug a tunnel under the Confederate lines and filled it with explosives. The ensuing explosion created a large crater, which the Union troops stormed into. Unfortunately, the crater had steep walls, and the soldiers found themselves trapped. It was very difficult to climb back out. They were shot down like fish in a barrel.

While in fact the whole affair turned into an unmitigated disaster— General Grant called it a "stupendous failure"—it would have been brilliant had the federal high command not frittered away the tremendous advantage of surprise. The sales lesson I derive is the value of the unanticipated solution. The mining of the Confederate lines actually was a great example of thinking outside the box and coming up with a solution that was as clever as it was unexpected.

**WHAT HAPPENED**

During the Siege of Petersburg, a group of Pennsylvania coal miners turned Union soldiers in Major General Ambrose Burnside's command developed a cunning plan to breach the Confederate lines. The labyrinth of defensive trenches had proven unassailable, and Union frustration was high in the hot summer months of 1864. Under the able direction of Lieutenant Colonel Henry Pleasants, who was himself a mining engineer before joining the army, the miners dug a tunnel 511 feet from the Union trenches to the middle of the Confederate lines. They then stacked 320 kegs, each loaded with 25 pounds of coarse gunpowder, in the galleries they had cleared 20 feet below the Confederate defenses. When the four tons of blasting powder was exploded at 4:45 a.m. on July 30, 1864, it blew a column of flame 200 feet in the air and created a crater 130 feet long, 75 feet wide, and 30 feet deep.

While the crater was not precisely what the Union command had expected, the explosion had caught the defenders completely unawares and had destroyed a third of the South Carolina brigade that was defending the position. It was the best opportunity yet to breach the

Confederate defenses and capture the Petersburg railroad station, which was so important to the defense of Richmond.

Major General Burnside had intended to use his 4th Division under Brigadier General Edward Ferrero—which was made up of nine regiments of fresh United States Colored Troops (USCT)—to lead the attack. This plan had been rejected by the commander of the Army of the Potomac, Major General George Meade, who was no doubt alive to the possible political repercussions if failure were to ensue. Apparently, this overruling drove Burnside into some kind of a depression, and rather than make a decision regarding the spearhead of the attack, he let his general officers draw lots for the privilege. The lot fell to Brigadier General James Ledlie, who was commander of the worn-out 1st Division and a known drunk. The mission was vitally important. If the assault succeeded in taking the high ground around Blandford Cemetery, the Union would be within artillery range of Petersburg. Moreover, General Lee's army would be divided.

As it turned out, Ledlie failed to pass the attack orders to his brigade commanders. In fact, he seems to have told them *not* to attack but rather to wait for the 4th Division to enter the fray. He may have been drunk.

By 7:00 a.m., two hours after the explosion, three divisions of Burnside's IX Corps were stuffed in and around the crater, which had by now become a shooting gallery. The Confederates had rallied sufficiently to bring up guns and block a Union breakout. At 8:00 a.m., when the day already seemed lost, Burnside sent in the USCT 4th Division. The troops fought well and gained some ground, but by 9:00 a.m., Brigadier General William Mahone arrived with rebel reinforcements and counterattacked. Brutal hand-to-hand fighting continued for several more hours before the rebels regained control of the salient.

The unanticipated solution provided by the genius of the Pennsylvania miners had been squandered; the Union had failed to take the heights along the Jerusalem Plank Road and end the siege. What could have been a spectacular victory, possibly ending the Civil War before Christmas of 1864, turned into one of the great disasters of the war. Almost 4,000 Union casualties, many of whom were USCTs who had been brutally murdered even after the legitimate fighting was over, attest to the terrible failure of Union leadership to capitalize on the extraordinary opportunity they had been given. *Ab obice saevior ibit.*

**WHAT IT MEANT**   The Battle of the Crater may have been Grant's best opportunity to end the siege of Petersburg. But alas, it failed. The stalemate and trench warfare continued for another eight very difficult months. While Pleasants was officially commended for the idea in principle, Burnside was relieved of command and sent on leave (he never did receive another command), and Ledlie was essentially dismissed from the army (he resigned his commission in January 1865).

**SALES LESSON**   The great lesson that makes this battle particularly memorable with regard to selling has to do with the unanticipated solution. It is the second of the four drivers that can help you to bring extraordinary value to your customer. As the miners had come up with an out-of-the-box idea for achieving their goal of breaching the rebel lines, so must the salesperson who is seeking to bring excellent value to the customer come up with a previously unimagined solution to the customer's problem.

The strict definition of identifying the unanticipated solution in Huthwaite parlance is this: Help the customer chart a better solution or achieve a better outcome.

The customer has a clear and present need and has charted a course to a desirable outcome. But the customer's solution may not be optimal. The job of the salesperson is to help the customer either chart a better course or achieve a more desirable outcome. When I talked about the unrecognized problem in Chapter 5, I was trying to get the customer to discover or redefine a problem; when I talk about the unanticipated solution, I am trying to get the customer to redefine the connective tissue between the problem and the outcome—or redefine the outcome.

Three conditions are necessary for a salesperson to be able to bring to bear an unanticipated solution on a sale. First, the customer must be aware of the problem or need and must feel the pain. Second, the customer must have already mapped out a possible solution to the problem. And finally, the customer must be crystal clear on the desired outcome. When these conditions have been met, it is possible for the salesperson to bring tremendous value to the customer by presenting a new, out-of-the-box solution to the problem or by presenting a better outcome.

But how can one come up with a better idea than the customer, who faces the problem every day, can come up with? And what is a better path to the outcome anyway? The better solution may be cheaper, faster, more beautiful, or something else. The better outcome may be more robust, more profitable, and so on. The answer lies in the ability of the salesperson to bring to the table a broader perspective, a wider outlook, a more encompassing vision. The salesperson may be able to see the problem from 30,000 feet, whereas the customer may be down in the weeds, trying to handle the problem reactively.

The salesperson must bring to bear his or her business acumen, industry knowledge, and questioning skills to help the customer come to the correct decision regarding the solution or the outcome on his or her own.

In the case of the unanticipated solution, the business acumen that will most come into play is the salesperson's understanding of the very basic business taxonomy, the five financial measures that are the foundation of every commercial enterprise:

- *Revenue.* How much money did the company generate in sales?
- *Cost of sales.* What did it cost the company to generate that revenue?
- *Margin.* How much money is the company making from what it's selling?
- *Expense.* What does it cost to run the business?
- *Profit.* What does the company put in its pocket?

It is incumbent on the salesperson to intimately understand these basic financial measures and how they work and, more to the point, to be intimately familiar with how his or her product or service can affect any or all of them.

Industry knowledge, looked at through the lens of these five measures, also will play an important part in allowing the salesperson to see solutions and outcomes with a fresh perspective. The particular knowledge that matters here is how other customers, dealing with some of the same problems, have met and overcome their problems. It also takes a strong capacity to recognize patterns—the ability to see how disparate parts play together in a coherent whole.

As I pointed out in Chapter 1, there is no substitute for preparation. There is no substitute for organizing and codifying all your industry knowledge and using your understanding of business processes to make assumptions and map out potential solutions for your customer's problems. A good salesperson will have already reached certain conclusions—from experience—about the customer's problems and intended solutions before he or she even meets with the customer.

When finally in front of the customer, the salesperson, who can make sense of a balance sheet and understands financial measures, can read the specifications plotted by the customer with one eye always on the outcome. He or she can determine when a specification is excellent and, more to the point, when it is not. He or she can see where and how each aspect of the plan affects the outcome in terms of the business fundamentals. The salesperson brings his or her expertise to bear and charts the superior course.

At this point, the salesperson engages the subtlety of questioning skills. Herein lies the vitality of the SPIN model. As we have seen, it is important that the customer reach his or her own conclusions. The skilled salesperson, seeing the objective, is able to lead the customer to that objective through careful questioning. He or she allows the customer to find the path himself or herself by sharing insight in the form of questions.

And the salesperson discovers, to his or her delight, that the customer is willing to pay handsomely for the insight.

The Union Army at the Battle of the Crater did not achieve the excellent results that were made possible by the brilliance of the unanticipated solution the miners had presented. But that was just poor execution of an outstanding path that had been opened up. It does not take away from the basic truth of the lesson that the unanticipated solution brings extraordinary value to the customer. *Ab obice saevior ibit.*

# 7

## BATTLE OF CLONTARF BRIAN BORU VERSUS THE VIKINGS (1014)

### THE VALUE DRIVERS: THE UNSEEN OPPORTUNITY

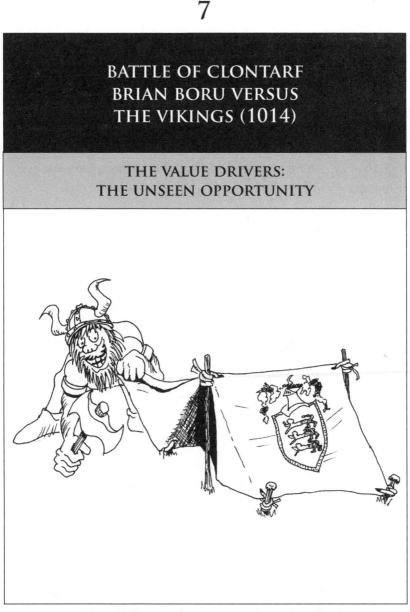

*I was seldom able to see an opportunity until it had ceased to be one.*
—MARK TWAIN

At the Battle of Clontarf in 1014, Brian Boru, the last High King of Ireland, led his forces against a combined force of Irish rebels and Viking mercenaries led by the King of Leinster, Máel Mórda mac Murchada. The loyal Irish routed the opposition, but Brian Boru was murdered in his tent by a couple of Vikings who came across him while fleeing the battlefield.

The sales lesson is on the importance of the *unseen opportunity* as a driver of value for the customer. While I do not necessarily support flight from a good fight, I approve wholly of grabbing an opportunity by the throat.

**WHAT HAPPENED**

Brian Boru (which translated means "Brian of the cattle tributes") is a legendary hero and great patriot of Ireland. Born a nobleman, a prince of the Dal Cais clan of southern Ireland around AD 940 (his father was King of Munster), he grew up witnessing wave after wave of Viking incursions into his ancestral home. He disliked the Danes from the start but learned to hate them passionately after he witnessed the murder of his mother by a roving band of Norse raiders. He began a policy of driving out every Dane he could lay his fingers on.

In 978, Brian succeeded his brother and comrade-in-arms Mathuin as King of Munster and united many of the tribes of southern Ireland.

By 1002, at a bit over 60 years of age, Brian was powerful enough to march on Tara—the grand old seat of Celtic kings. He forced Malachy, King of the Ui Neill, to abdicate and took the title High King of Ireland. Irish culture flourished under his benign rule. His kingship was largely symbolic because the tribes of the island and the feudal system that governed the clans precluded any sort of national government. Nevertheless, he was a great patron of the arts and did much to preserve Irish literature; he also helped to rebuild monasteries and stocked them with books.

In 1012, Máel Mórda mac Murchada, King of Leinster, revolted against Brian Boru's rule. Mael Morda joined forces with Sigtrygg Silkbeard, Danish King of Dublin, and the rebellion became general. Brian tried a bizarre series of marriage alliances to quell the uprising by diplomatic means, but his attempts at a peaceful resolution failed. War broke out, which culminated at the Battle of Clontarf on April 23, 1014.

This legendary battle pitted the rebel force of Mael Morda's Irish Leistermen and other assorted Irish rebels from various clans, Sigtrygg's Dublin Vikings, a contingent under Sigurd—the Viking earl of the Orkney Isles—and the Viking warriors of Brodir of the Isle of Man against Brian Boru's army of loyal Irish troops and a contingent of foreign (Viking) mercenaries. It was all very complicated, really.

The Battle of Clontarf began early on that Good Friday morning with a series of personal challenges and the resulting individual clashes in the no-man's land between the armies to settle grudges and family feuds. As these private wars were fought in earnest, the armies began slowly moving forward toward one another. They eventually clashed and the battle proper began. Brodir of Man apparently fought bravely and to great effect until a formidable Irish warrior called Wolf the Quarrelsome found him and felled him with a couple of blows, after which Brodir fled ingloriously into the woods.

The battle raged hour after hour. Eventually, the loyal Irish forces with their mercenary Viking cohorts set the Leistermen and their allies to flight and achieved final victory.

Brian Boru, by now in his seventies, did not actually participate in the fight. After riding in front of his army and delivering a rousing speech before the battle, he retired to the rear to pray for victory in his tent. Incredibly, the cowardly Brodir of Man and a few of his warriors stumbled on the lightly guarded tent, killed the retainers, and then dispatched Brian Boru with an axe. Brodir and his men were soon captured and executed on the orders of Wolf the Quarrelsome.

Both sides took extraordinarily high casualties, and both lost almost all their leaders in the battle. It remains one of the bloodiest battles in the history of Ireland.

**WHAT IT MEANT**

The Battle of Clontarf abruptly ended the many years of Viking destructive power in Ireland. In the years following Clontarf, Viking raiders and invaders focused on England and Scotland rather than Ireland. But, of course, at that point the Vikings had been in Ireland for nearly two centuries and had in many ways melded with their Celtic brethren. They had taken Irish wives and settled in for the long haul. The two cultures were already becoming assimilated.

The battle also effectively ended the High Kingship of Ireland and any hope for a real monarchy. Brian Boru was the first true (mostly) King of Ireland and most certainly the last. The clans fell back into the ancient patterns of in-fighting until the Anglo-Norman invasion ended all that the following century.

In the late Middle Ages, noble families that could not point to an ancestor who had fought and died bravely at Clontarf were not considered really noble after all. Songs, poems, and sagas celebrate the glory that is Clontarf. And the prominent Irish O'Brien clan traces its roots to Brian Boru.

**SALES LESSON**

The tragic if kingly death of Brian Boru reminds us of the importance of the *unseen opportunity* as a value driver in sales. The Viking Brodir of the Isle of Man spotted the otherwise unseen opportunity to kill the king at the Battle of Clontarf. Ignoble, yes—and cowardly—but an apt reminder of the lesson.

The third value driver is this: The seller creates or reveals an unseen opportunity for the buyer or the buyer's organization. Exploring the unseen opportunity is about helping the customer imagine opportunities that he or she otherwise would not consider.

Business executives are paid to produce the outcome that is desirable but not inevitable. And it is not always about solving problems, at least not the customer's problems. Regarding the unrecognized problem and the unanticipated solution, the seller is asked to consider his or her customer's problems—those of which they are unaware and those of which they are all too painfully aware. With the unseen opportunity, by contrast, the seller is being asked to consider the problems being experienced by the customer's customer. This is to say, the seller is being asked to seek new ways for the customer to serve the marketplace. What can the customer do to expand his or her client base or open up a new client base.

It is important to note that the unseen opportunity will not bring the business down if it is not adopted. It is a nice-to-have, not a must-have. Failure to exploit the opportunity will not have a negative impact on the business. The upside of a good opportunity is enormous, though, and potentially will expand the customer's marketplace. While providing value for the customer, it also generally will be good for the seller.

A stellar example of passing along an unseen opportunity is seen in the man who sold engine oil to United Parcel Service (UPS). He had noticed in his dealings with the giant parcel delivery service that the company was exceptionally adept at logistics and fleet maintenance. He suggested to UPS that it consider getting into the business of logistics and fleet maintenance consulting. So the company did, and a multimillion-dollar consulting business was born at UPS. It expanded the company's business into new territory and created a whole new customer base—but it was not strictly necessary to the core business of parcel delivery, which was doing just fine without a consulting arm. It was above and beyond. Value creation happens when a seller helps a customer to discover an untapped capability.

The discovery by the seller of an unseen opportunity is not an easy process and is often helped along by just a touch of luck. But remember: Chance favors only the prepared mind. Finding the unseen opportunity depends on a prepared mind. Once again, the discovery lies at the intersection of business acumen, industry knowledge, and questioning skill.

Knowledgeable questioning can lead the customer through a process of self-discovery; it can help the customer to see his or her company's capabilities in a new light. It can help the customer to consider areas of the business that are unused or underleveraged in the marketplace. And through the questioning process, new ideas may occur to the seller and/ or to the customer about how those capabilities might be exploited to expand the existing client base or open up a new market.

Industry knowledge in the case of the unseen opportunity is of a more general sort. It is of a broad and comprehensive sort. It is knowledge of the competitive landscape across a wide horizon. The salesman who sold oil to UPS understood the marketplace. He was alive to the possibility that the core strengths of the company could be leveraged competitively. His clarity of vision allowed him to see potentiality because he knew what the market could use and in the end needed.

Business acumen also plays a vital role in the discovery of unseen opportunities. Most unseen opportunities are shared at the upper level of management and generally in the C-suite. It is extremely important that a salesperson be able to speak the language of the executive suite— which is, in short, the five key business metrics discussed in Chapter 6: revenue, cost of sales, margin, expense, and profit. The salesperson who can see what plays into these measures in the business of his or her customer is the salesperson who is prepared to discover and help the customer discover the unseen opportunity. This kind of business acumen and understanding of the customer's business establishes trust. To find those core capabilities that might be exploited, the seller must consider those aspects of the customer's business that outsourcing would not improve. In other words, what capabilities that are auxiliary to the customer's main business does the customer do so well that outside help would not improve the situation? These are the capabilities that are fraught with the potential for exploitation in the marketplace.

The confluence of business acumen, industry knowledge, and questioning skill provides the fertile ground for exploring unseen opportunities. It also forms the basis of the prepared mind. When a seller is able to separate the core capability that makes a business successful from the enabling competencies that make it possible, he or she is on the road to discovery of an unseen opportunity. It is important to recognize that discovery of an unseen opportunity is not easy. It is not an everyday occurrence. In fact, the salesperson who can offer just a few unseen opportunities to customers over a lifetime of selling ought to consider himself or herself lucky.

Unlike the unrecognized problem and the unanticipated solution, one cannot develop a cheat sheet for the unseen opportunity. Unrecognized problems and unanticipated solutions can be collected, if you will. They can be gathered together, studied, and delivered across an industry. A given unrecognized problem may plague a whole variety of businesses—and is only unrecognized by the customer who is suffering. The salesperson clearly recognizes the problem from experience. The same goes for the unanticipated solution. A particular solution may well apply to every business operating in a particular space. Not so the unseen opportunity. A particular opportunity generally applies only once to a single customer. But it is a game changer.

As mentioned earlier, discovery of an unseen opportunity may depend to some degree on luck. As with the Viking Brodir of the Isle of Man—an unseen opportunity may occur only once—and that once by pure coincidence. But, as with Brodir, the great thing is to be ready to seize the opportunity when it presents itself. *Aut nunc, aut numquam.* It is incumbent on the savvy salesperson to be prepared at all times for any eventuality in the delivery of excellent value to the customer.

# 8

### THE VALUE DRIVERS:
### THE BROKER OF CAPABILITIES

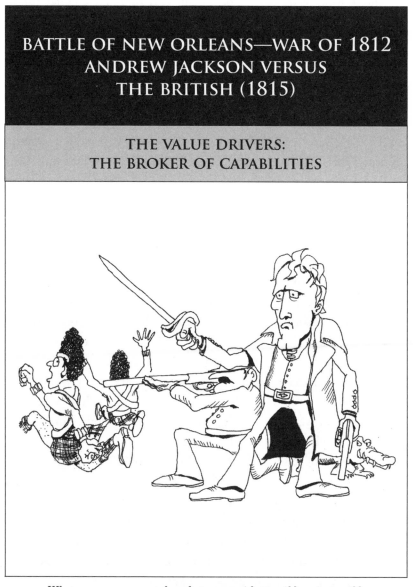

*What we can or cannot do, what we consider possible or impossible,*
*is rarely a function of our true capability. It is more likely a*
*function of our beliefs about who we are.*
—TONY ROBBINS

The Battle of New Orleans, regarded as Andrew Jackson's finest hour, took place at the end of the War of 1812. The defense of New Orleans was critical to American interests because its loss might result in the loss of the vast Louisiana territory that Thomas Jefferson had purchased from Napoleon in 1803 for $15 million. The Americans were "all in." Andrew Jackson was betting America's future on the success of this venture, so he brokered his capabilities. He brought Jean Lafitte—the notorious privateer with an American price on his head— and Lafitte's Baratarian fighting men with 7,500 flints and powder into his army. The Baratarians were a contributing factor to Jackson's stunning victory over the British.

Jackson brought to bear all available resources; he augmented his forces with smugglers and freebooters. The sales lesson is on the final value driver: the *broker of capabilities*.

**WHAT HAPPENED**

On January 8, 1815, a most extraordinary army under the leadership of Major General Andrew Jackson crushed a British invasion force that was threatening New Orleans, the Mississippi, and the hopes of a fledgling American republic. In 1812, President James Madison asked the U.S. Congress to declare war on Great Britain over the question of neutrality rights on the high seas. The British, who were in the throes of war with France, had an annoying habit of impressing American merchant seaman into service in the Royal Navy. For the first couple of years of the war, England all but ignored the upstart Americans. But then, after success in the Peninsular War, now that Napoleon was nearly defeated, Britain finally turned its full attention to the war with the United States in 1814. The British worked out a three-pronged attack in force. The first part of the invasion force would attack the Hudson Valley and Lake Champlain in the North through Canada; the second part would concentrate on the great port of Baltimore and the new U.S. capital at Washington, DC, through the Chesapeake Bay, and the third part would attack the southern coast of the United States— most likely at New Orleans.

The northern campaign ultimately failed. As did the Chesapeake campaign—although the British did defeat the Americans at the Battle of Bladensburg and subsequently burned Washington, DC, they nevertheless failed to take Baltimore. British hopes now were pinned on the southern campaign.

In preparation for the defense of New Orleans, General Jackson gathered a ragtag army that was centered on the U.S. 7th Infantry—a hard-drinking but tough regiment that had been put together several years earlier by future president Zachary Taylor. He recruited the local militia, some Choctaw Indians, some Creoles, some Spaniards, a number of free African-Americans, and small companies of riflemen from Tennessee, Kentucky, and Louisiana—pretty much every able-bodied laborer, frontiersman, and sailor in New Orleans was tapped.

Perhaps the most interesting recruit was the famous privateer Jean Lafitte and his private army of pirates and freebooters, known as Baratarians after their stronghold in Barataria Bay 30 miles south of New Orleans. Governor Clairborne of Louisiana had recently sent forces to raid Barataria Bay and in so doing had reduced Lafitte's fortune considerably. In addition, he had captured and jailed Lafitte's brother, Pierre. Lafitte was approached by the British in September of 1814 to join their expedition against New Orleans, but in the end he asked for and got pardons for himself and his Baratarians on condition that they serve with the American defenders.

General Jackson prepared his defenses about six miles down the Mississippi from New Orleans at the Chalmette Plantation. The Americans built a line of breastworks along a mill stream known as Canal Rodriguez that separated Chalmette from the Macarty Plantation. The line was about a mile long—known to the men as "Line Jackson"—running east to west from a cypress swamp (on the advice of Jean Lafitte) all the way to the river. Jackson's seriously heterogeneous army now totaled some 4,000 men. They would stand against some 8,000 seasoned British Redcoats, some of whom were veterans of the Peninsular Campaign in Spain. *Virtus, non copia vincint.*

On the morning of January 8, the British advanced through fog toward the American defenses. Artillery on both sides opened up. British cannonballs smashed harmlessly into the muddy ramparts of Line Jackson, whereas American cannonballs mowed down the advancing Redcoats. It was a general slaughter. The British did manage to almost reach the breastworks on the right flank of the American lines, defended by the 7th Infantry, but were repelled by murderous fire from a small cadre of Louisiana riflemen.

Led by commanding privateers Dominique You and Renato Beluche, the Baratarians apparently conducted themselves with admirable bravery and steadiness. They were, of course, used to fighting together on pirate ships and were no strangers to the violence of battle. Still, General Jackson made a point of noting their gallantry as bombardiers and credited their excellent manning of several artillery pieces.

The battle was over by midmorning, the fields strewn with more than 2,000 British dead and wounded. The Americans had won decisively in a very short time. Jackson's most unusual amalgamation of unlikely warriors had suffered only 70 casualties, 13 of which were dead.

**WHAT IT MEANT**

The Battle of New Orleans was the last great battle of the War of 1812. In fact, it happened after the Treaty of Ghent had been signed, ending the war. News of the peace agreement had not yet reached New Orleans. The battle secured the Gulf Coast of the United States and excited a tremendous feeling of national identity in Americans. Andrew Jackson's unlikely army had utterly destroyed a powerful invasion force from the strongest nation on earth. It was a famous victory and quite an accomplishment. One could argue that in the end it was this victory that eventually propelled General Jackson into the White House as the seventh president of the United States in 1829.

**SALES LESSON**

Andrew Jackson made full use of every available resource to handle the defense of New Orleans. He took all that the city had to offer and molded it into an effective fighting force. In short, he acted as a broker of capabilities. We call the fourth value driver in the salesperson's arsenal the *broker of capabilities*—whereby the seller serves to make available to the buyer the full range of capabilities of the seller's organization in such a way that these capabilities contribute to an expansion or redefinition of the customer's success. In short, brokering capabilities turns out to be effective cross-selling.

The notion that it is far less taxing to expand share-of-wallet with existing customers through cross-selling than it is to find new customers is almost a truism. In today's hypercompetitive markets, several trends have emerged that are energizing cross-selling initiatives across most industries. First, many industries are going through a period of consolidation on a massive scale. Industries such as banking, enterprise technology, and medical equipment serve as prime examples of this consolidation. In addition, Wall Street demands organic growth within public companies. Finally, in an extrapolation of Moore's law to broader industry, new products and services are being developed at a much faster rate than ever before.

The first and most important driving force of cross-selling has emanated from the fact that every industry has followed the same accelerating trajectory—an ongoing consolidation of suppliers. There are two primary reasons that businesses are consolidating: (1) They seek to gain economies of scale, and (2) they seek to create a market presence.

With all this consolidation has come a spate of cross-selling initiatives. As companies merge, they find that they have customers who do not enjoy all the benefits of their new offerings, and companies seek to change this.

The second important factor in the increase in cross-selling initiatives is an extrapolation of Moore's law. In 1965, Gordon Moore (director of Research and Development Laboratories, Fairchild Semiconductor Division, Fairchild Camera and Instrument Corp.) observed that the number of transistors on an integrated circuit doubles every two years (later updated to every 18 months). While Moore was looking at the empirical reality of transistor technology, the law does have a wider applicability. That is to say, the surge in product development and expansion across industries has been exponential. If not actually doubling every two years, everything from crop-development technologies, to new drugs, to plasma-screen televisions, to enterprise software integration techniques seems to be improving and increasing at a very rapid pace. This means that most industries have more and better products to offer all the time. As companies increase their product offerings, cross-selling becomes absolutely necessary to survive against the competition that is already or soon afterwards flogging the same improvements.

The third reason that cross-selling is on the rise is that many business leaders in sales and marketing organizations are being tasked with expanding market share organically (as opposed to growing externally by merger or acquisition) and as quickly as possible. They are supposed to accomplish this organic growth within the context of markets that are constantly changing: consolidating suppliers, consolidating customers, new capabilities/product advancements by competitors, and external market forces that are well beyond a business leader's power to control.

For many sales leaders in this situation, the idea of developing new markets or new clients from scratch is a nonstarter. There simply isn't enough time or enough resources to invest. Most industry analyses show that it costs five to eight times more to acquire a new customer than to retain a current one. And what's more, the cost of losing a customer must include all the hidden costs of lifetime potential spending and bad press. Anyone who has been in professional sales for more than 10 minutes is intuitively aware of these realities. From a business standpoint, then, it makes sense not only to do what's necessary to retain current customers but also to expand relationships with those customers. Many business leaders feel that if a customer relationship is not advancing, then it soon will be retreating. For these leaders, cross-selling strategies represent the only path to achieving the goal of achieving organic growth in the face of such daunting market challenges.

In addition to the obvious appeal for sellers, there are advantages for their customers as well, who ostensibly can address needs that exist within their businesses simply by tapping more deeply into the capabilities of providers whom they already trust. Customers also can achieve greater economies of scale with key suppliers that help them to reduce several different areas of cost all at once. The *advertised* intent of cross-selling initiatives today often includes real, positive outcomes for both sellers and buyers alike.

And yet, unluckily, cross-selling has gotten a bad name with customers because it is done improperly, indelicately, or just plain ineptly. It often makes the customer angry because it is focused more on the selfish desire of the seller to sell than on the needs of the customer. Often, cross-selling is not done in the spirit of *mutual benefit*.

Cross-selling initiatives generally fail for one (or both) of two reasons:

1. Risk aversion
2. Flawed business logic

## RISK AVERSION

Many salespeople are resistant to cross-selling because it is inherently risky. In many cases there is no upside to the original seller for bringing in a colleague. There is *only* risk. If things don't go well, the business relationship the original seller already has is going to be shaken, and if things go fabulously well and they make the cross-sell, there's nothing in it for the original seller. Even if a small incentive is involved, it is simply not worth the risk of losing a great relationship.

Of course, this is all based on ill-considered logic and a degree of myopia; it comes from the perspective of things the original seller wants to sell instead of from the perspective of the value he or she wants to create. Thus the way to conquer risk aversion on the part of the original seller (who has the existing relationship with the customer) is to bring value creation to the fore. When one creates value, even through a colleague, the differentiation accrues to the whole relationship. Thus the original seller really does win. If real value is created, the buyer naturally will be appreciative, and the relationship bonds will grow stronger on all fronts. By approaching cross-selling from the standpoint of *creating value* instead of *selling*, the original seller is credited with success.

## FLAWED BUSINESS LOGIC

Virtually every industry is enduring some degree of commoditization. The flow and availability of information to buyers about prospective suppliers are making it more difficult for sellers to distinguish themselves from their competition. Customer-procurement strategies are being designed to force suppliers to compete on one lone criterion—price.

For many firms, the path out of this difficult reality runs straight through their existing customer base. Rather than fight the often unrewarding battle of convincing new customers that they're not only competitively different but also *valuable*, these organizations look to expand their relationships with existing customers who seemingly already perceive some value in their capabilities. The very existence of a business relationship seems evidence enough of the kind of perceived value that can be traded like currency to get access to new areas of the customer's business.

Unfortunately, many business and sales leaders who choose to embark on company-wide cross-selling initiatives are operating under the flawed assumption that this *currency* is worth a great deal more than it really is. In many cases it amounts to nothing more than fool's gold.

Huthwaite's founder, Neil Rackham, wrote about the role of sellers in the creation of value for customers in the book, *Rethinking the Sales Force* (McGraw-Hill, New York, 1999). He states: "Today's sales forces can no longer exist in isolation. . . . Instead, they must be an integral part of the company's value creation and value delivery chain."

Ineffective cross-selling initiatives fail because they turn the idea of the *sales force as part of the value-creation and value-delivery chain* squarely on its head. They frequently pit what is good for the selling organization against what is good for the buyer, essentially forcing sellers to offer expanded capabilities without first helping buyers to gain insight into new opportunities they can seize or new challenges they can address.

In its proper orientation, today's business value chain starts from the perspective of the customer or the market. It is for this reason that sellers in today's market have such a vital role in establishing competitive differentiation for their organizations. Without the seller functioning as the eyes and ears of a business's value-delivery chain, vital functions such as product fulfillment, service delivery, manufacturing, and research and development (R&D) are essentially blind and deaf.

The first job in effective cross-selling is to realize that to broker capabilities, the proper mind-set is not "I've got a truck full of products, and I want to sell them all to you." Rather, it's a mind-set that thinks in terms of customers with a splendid array of needs, all of which must be communicated and understood effectively within the seller's company so that the company as a whole can meet as many of those needs as possible.

We must remember that effective selling hinges on understanding and addressing only the needs that customers recognize as worthy of action. Once this foundation is established, effective cross-sellers turn their focus toward helping customers understand additional problems or opportunities that one's organization can tackle. The success of cross-selling then hinges on one's ability to help customers draw the conclusion that those problems or opportunities are important enough to warrant taking action and furthering the relationship.

If you build your cross-selling plan around that idea of customer problems you can solve or opportunities you can help customers to seize, then you're coming from the market perspective. With this in mind, the following steps need to be taken:

1. You need to develop some mechanism by which the seller who is inside an account can begin to assemble an understanding of the needs and opportunities that may present themselves and the needs and opportunities that the customer doesn't see.

2. You need to develop a cross-selling plan within your company. This plan needs to be derived from the spectrum of problems and opportunities you've identified: Where are the places that you can meet the needs or seize the opportunities? Be mindful of how you can position yourself uniquely in terms of the incumbent competition and those who may compete for the business.

3. Finally, prioritize your planned problems and opportunities in the context of who you know inside the account who would be most receptive to the original message? Who internal to the customer can coach you on how to refine your understanding of the competitive landscape? And who inside the account do you need to begin to talk to?

In short, effective cross-selling is *not* about starting with products and deciding where they could be sold. It's about starting with the customer and deciding what needs you can meet.

# 9

## ON PRESCRIPTION BEFORE DIAGNOSIS

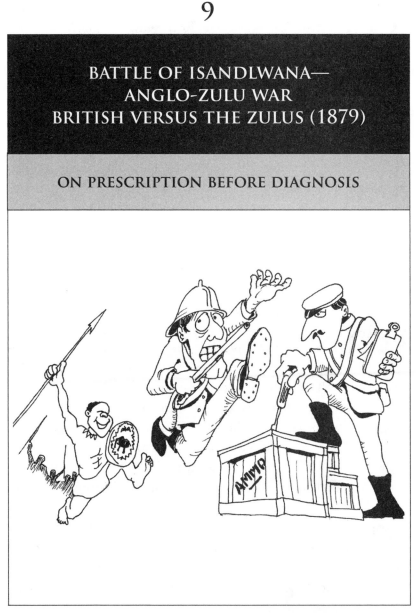

*Bedside manners are no substitute for the right diagnosis.*
—ALFRED P. SLOAN, CHAIRMAN OF GENERAL MOTORS, 1937–1956

The Battle of Isandlwana was the first major encounter between the British and the Zulus after the British invaded Zululand. It was a contest of vastly superior numbers (12:1) against vastly superior arms (traditional Assegai iron spears against then state-of-the-art Martini-Henry breech-loading rifles). Numbers won. The British were humiliated in a crushing defeat. The powerful British colonial officer who had conceived the affair had not really thought things through. He considered the Zulus a threat to Natal and ordered an invasion without properly diagnosing the threat. His army charged into Zululand in ox carts, ready for a quick and decisive victory against the natives. His prescription for an improperly diagnosed threat was a dismal failure.

In sales, you have to really understand the problem or threat to a client organization before you come leaping in with answers that may or may not meet the case. As in medicine, prescription without proper diagnosis is malpractice.

**WHAT HAPPENED**

The Anglo-Zulu War of 1879 was the brainchild of Sir Henry Bartle Frère, the British High Commissioner in Natal. Zululand, which lay strategically between the British colonial territories of Natal and Transvaal, had become a most desirable geographic area after the discovery of diamonds in South Africa. Frère seems to have considered its continued independence a threat to British interests in the region. In December 1878, he decided to provoke a fight with Zulu King Cetshwayo kaMpande as a pretext for occupying Zululand. Although aware that the project ran against the general policy of Queen Victoria's government, which was already stretched thin and would be unlikely to support colonial expansion at that time, Frère reckoned that he could settle the matter before the Colonial Office ever got wind of it. He sent an ultimatum to the Zulu king that he knew would be rejected—which it was—and so sent an invasion force.

On January 11, 1879, under the command of Lieutenant General Frederick Thesiger, Second Baron Chelmsford, 5,000 British soldiers and about 500 African troops of the Natal Native Contingent crossed the Buffalo River at Rorke's Drift into Zululand. Thus began one of the greatest and most improbable disasters in British colonial history.

The invasion force made incredibly slow progress toward the Zulu capital at Ulundi because the supply wagons were pulled by teams of oxen. By January 20, Chelmsford's force had advanced only 10 miles and set up camp beneath a peculiar rock formation known as Isandlwana. While Chelmsford rested his men, he sent Major John Dartnell with a contingent of mounted police on an intelligence-gathering expedition. Dartnell encountered a small band of several hundred Zulu warriors. He reported the discovery and requested reinforcements. Chelmsford, believing they had found the main Zulu army, set out in the early morning of January 22 with 2,500 men and four guns to attack the Zulus. This was Chelmsford's first fatal blunder: He committed the cardinal error of dividing his force.

He left the remainder of the British troops and a couple hundred of the Natal Native Contingent at Isandlwana in the charge of a battalion commander named Lieutenant Colonel Henry Pulleine. He also sent orders to Brevet Colonel Anthony Durnford to bring up the 2nd Column, which he had left at Rorke's Drift. His orders, however, were vague, and Durnford was unclear as to whether he was meant to reinforce the camp at Isandlwana or Chelmsford himself. Durnford decided on the latter and prepared to move out to protect Chelmsford's rear.

This left about 1,700 British troops in camp at Isandlwana. The camp was just a bunch of soldiers and their tents out in the open. There was no protection whatsoever. The usual and proper approach to encampment in South Africa was to *laager*, or circle the wagons. Chelmsford, however, was supremely overconfident in the received colonial wisdom that no native army could defeat a British force. The British were quite simply superior, both in technology and in fighting capability. The Zulu *impi* (army) would absolutely collapse under the withering firepower of the breech-loading Martini-Henry rifle. No need to *laager*.

As it turned out, King Cetshwayo was no lightweight. He had understood the implied threat in Frère's ultimatum and had moved quickly to rally an army in defense of his land. He mustered some 25,000 warriors who, under the command of *Inkhosi* (General) Ntshingwayo kaMohole, advanced against the British invasion force. While the Zulu *Inkhosi* kept the main army together in force, he did send out a few small diversionary bands of warriors. The diversion worked because it caused Chelmsford to foolishly divide his force and leave his camp grossly undermanned and unprotected.

The camp at Isandlwana was ripe for the picking. The Zulu plan was to attack at dawn on January 23, but a Lieutenant Charles Raw discovered the encampment of the main Zulu army just a few miles from Isandlwana. He sent runners to warn Lieutenant Colonel Pulleine, but it was too late. Twenty thousand well-trained and disciplined Zulu warriors descended on the terribly unprepared British camp.

The battle began just after noon on January 22, 1879. The Zulus attacked in their traditional buffalo formation, in which the forces divided into "horns" to the right and left of the main army, which made up the "chest" in the center. The horns were designed to enclose the enemy flanks.

The 24th Regiment of Foot, under Lieutenant Colonel Pulleine, formed up several hundred yards from the camp. Durnford's Royal Engineers were way off to the right of the British line when the shooting started. It was almost as though there were two separate battles going on. The line was way overextended and massively undermanned. Nevertheless, the 24th Infantry comported itself with its usual valor and tremendous discipline. They opened fire with their Martini-Henry rifles from about 600 yards, sending volley after volley slowly and deliberately and with devastating effect into the Zulu ranks.

After about half an hour, the tide began to turn in favor of the Zulus. A partial eclipse of the sun brought a strange semidarkness to the battlefield just as Durford's men ran out of ammunition and started to fall back. Simultaneously, the Natal Native Contingent turned tail and fled while the right horn of the *impi* crashed into the British left. It was all over but the shouting.

Only 5 British officers survived the Battle of Isandlwana and some 50 soldiers—all of whom escaped on horseback. It was a complete, utter, and humiliating defeat for the British. *Bona diagnosis, bona curatio.*

**WHAT IT MEANT**

British imperial power had been tweaked, and the British public was not amused. Popular support for colonialism rose to a fever pitch in an otherwise staid Victorian England. Revenge against the Zulus was the cry that went round the countryside. A relief expedition under Sir Garnet Wolseley was mustered, but as it turned out, Lord Chelmsford was able finally to defeat the Zulus at the Battle of Ulundi on July 4, 1879, before Wolseley arrived. Chelmsford's fighting career nevertheless was over. Private Samuel Wassal, who survived Isandlwana, was awarded a Victoria Cross in recognition of bravery. Colonel Durnford was blamed for the disaster because he was dead and could not defend himself.

**SALES LESSON**

Sir Henry Bartle Frère had prescribed a war against the Zulus on the basis of an improper diagnosis. Salespeople should take note: It is never okay to prescribe the antidote before the diagnosis is made.

How many times have you heard it said: "Prescription without diagnosis is malpractice?" It is a platitude to be sure, but as it happens, it is true—across the board. And the troubling thing is that it happens all the time in every field of human endeavor (hopefully less in medicine than in other, less potentially mortal strivings). That is to say, even knowing that it is logically erroneous and, indeed, untenable, people are apt to prescribe without proper diagnosis.

How often do salespeople leap in with the solution before either they themselves or their customers completely understand the nature of the problem? In a recent Huthwaite survey of over 600 Fortune 500 sales managers, 72 percent said that their salespeople jump in with solutions before the customer has seen a need for one. This is a grave error.

Imagine being quite ill and going to the doctor for some relief. You step into the dreaded room, note that the doctor throws a cursory glance in your general direction, and then the doctor begins furiously scribbling a prescription for you. You might wonder just what on earth the doctor thinks he or she is basing the diagnosis on—you haven't even begun to describe your symptoms yet.

It happens all the time in sales training, for example. The sales manager arrives at the door of the training compatriot and says, "My people aren't hitting their numbers. We have to figure out a way to fix this. Find a way to help us meet our numbers." So the training person reaches into his or her file drawer and selects a folder entitled, "Sales Training." From the folder the trainer selects a sales training program, hopefully one of the less expensive varieties (because how different can they really be, after all?), and there it is—the prescription without diagnosis.

The trick to correct diagnosis is *data, not guesswork*. And as we have seen, data are garnered in a variety of ways. First, data are gathered the old-fashioned way—by just plain hard work and background research. Second, data are gained by experience. Industry knowledge and business acumen are developed over time by experience, and they become the salesperson's *expertise*. Finally, data are gained by asking the right questions.

*Expertise*, viewed through the lens of the customer's perspective, is key to driving value. But it is best shared by employing a particular form of diagnostic questioning. The word *diagnostic* cannot be overstated in this case. Merely asking questions may be a good way to get the buyer to talk, but in and of themselves, questions can become nothing more than a polite interrogation.

This is why sales calls and strategies that focus on products and services so often fail to connect with customers today. Bringing the value drivers alive requires conducting calls and strategies that help the customer draw conclusions, establish value expectations, and extend invitations to the seller to describe his or her offerings and capabilities. The key, again, is asking the right questions.

One needs to understand the full story—and one needs to elicit an invitation—before one can legitimately start spouting solutions.

Too often we come across salespeople who tend to leap to conclusions based on their experience or expertise rather than on the facts that would be presented given the chance. The problem is that they are genuinely brilliant. They may in fact know too much. So they do too little to understand the business of their clients—let alone their clients' specific issues and concerns. They rely instead on generalities that may or may not be appropriate in a given case. They tend in the end to merely communicate value rather than *create* value.

In a recent Huthwaite research project, we asked the following question: "Which description is most representative of how you are differentiated in the marketplace today?" Fifty-six percent of sales managers did *not* think "Our sales team is our value-creating differentiator in the marketplace" was the most desirable answer. In fact, a disturbing 40 percent preferred "Our sales force is good at communicating our value proposition and our product and solution differentiators in the marketplace" as the most desirable answer. Value communication is still seen as an acceptable approach to sales. *It is not!* There is simply no substitute anymore for creating value. And to do that, a salesperson must be able to ask the right questions in order to formulate the right diagnosis and then proceed forward.

# 10

## ON PREVENTING OBJECTIONS

*Nothing will ever be attempted if all possible objections must first be overcome.*
—SAMUEL JOHNSON

The gunfight at the OK Corral was fought in Tombstone, Arizona. It was five men ostensibly on the side of the law against four cowboys, two of whom were quite possibly unarmed. Although only three men were killed during the gunfight, it is generally regarded as the most famous gunfight in the history of the Old West. It was, in essence, a feud between Yankee carpetbaggers and Southern ranchers, some of them erstwhile friends or at least fellow gamblers. The dispute could have been defused fairly easily without bloodshed.

The lesson is that it is better to prevent objections rather than to handle objections. Once an objection is on the table in a negotiation, it is difficult to prevent some degree of antagonism. If the objections are prevented by doing a thorough job of selling during the sales process, they are unlikely to come up later during negotiations.

**WHAT HAPPENED**

On the cool and windy afternoon of October 26, 1881, perhaps the most famous gunfight in the history of the Old West took place in a vacant lot a block in front of the OK Corral in Tombstone, Arizona Territory. The battle has caused a century of hot dispute over who drew first, who shot whom, and which were the bad guys and which the good. It is indeed a tangled web—and I shall not try to untangle it except to say that the lines between good and bad do seem a bit blurry. It was really a battle between the new and the old, the Yankee carpetbaggers and the Southern ranchers; between the tinhorn gambling element, mining speculators and saloonkeepers, and the landowners, stockmen, and occasional rustlers. What it was not was cut and dried "goodies versus baddies." What it was was a deadly donnybrook that didn't have to happen.

The seeds of the conflict were sown over the months leading up to that fateful day. The so-called Cowboys (newspapers at the time used the capitalized term almost interchangeably with *rustlers*) were a loosely knit confederation of ranchers, horse thieves, and the occasional troubled gunfighter. Six stolen army mules, a failed stagecoach robbery, and several posse manhunts involving supposed Cowboys set accusations flying between Ike Clanton and notorious gambling drunk

John Henry "Doc" Holliday—who believed that Ike was threatening his friend Wyatt Earp. Earp was the faro banker at the Oriental Saloon and a former lawman. His older brother, Virgil, was the town marshal of Tombstone and his youngest brother, Morgan, was a deputy lawman.

After a heated verbal confrontation between an ornery Doc and an unarmed Ike at the Alhambra Saloon on the evening of October 25, death threats were made on both sides. Ike spent the night simmering and playing poker with Virgil Earp, Tom McLaury, Cochise County Sheriff Johnny Behan, and a fourth man. In the morning, Virgil and Johnny went to bed. Ike apparently kept drinking and wandering around town (now fully armed with his Winchester rifle and his revolver—which he had picked up from the West End Corral), supposedly looking for Holliday or any Earp to fight. Virgil was awakened around noon and warned of Ike's bar hopping and braggadocio. Virgil snuck up on Ike and pistol-whipped him, disarmed him, and arrested him on the charge of carrying deadly weapons within the limits of the City of Tombstone. Ike was fined $25 plus court fees and set free, unarmed. Virgil left the confiscated weapons at the Grand Hotel for Ike to retrieve when he was leaving town.

Wyatt had an unpleasant conversation with Ike in the courtroom and then, when leaving, happened on Tom McLaury, his erstwhile friend, who Wyatt thought to be armed. Wyatt tried to pick a fight (which apparently baffled poor Tom, who may well have been unarmed, even though he was in town to collect $3,000—much of it in cash—from the local butcher). In the end, Wyatt pistol-whipped young Tom and stalked off. He was apparently in no mood for confronting armed Cowboys. Rumors spread quickly and soon reached the ears of newly arrived Frank McLaury (Tom's brother) and Billy Clanton (Ike's popular 19-year-old brother). Wyatt seemed to be spoiling for a fight.

Virgil by this time had had quite enough of the threats and innuendoes and decided to put an end to it by disarming the Cowboys. He deputized Doc and Wyatt and gathered young Morgan, and the four of them set off down Fremont Street toward the area where the Cowboys were last reported seen. Virgil had Doc's walking stick in his right hand (to show that he wasn't looking for a fight); Doc had Virgil's sawed-off double-barreled shotgun hidden under his overcoat and a pistol to boot. Doc might have been looking for a fight. The Earps each had a revolver in his pocket or waistband.

Meanwhile, Sheriff Johnny Behan tried to disarm Frank McLaury. Frank refused, apparently insisting that the Earps be disarmed first. Behan then approached the Earps and allegedly told them that he had already disarmed the Cowboys. The Earps brushed passed him and continued on down to the vacant alleyway between Fly's photographic studio and a boarding house (where, incidentally, Doc Holliday was renting a room) and the MacDonald house.

Virgil then either told the Cowboys to "throw up your hands" or to "give up your arms" or something to that effect. Frank McLaury and Billy Clanton reached for their guns (whether to give them up or to shoot remains unclear), and immediately two shots rang out almost simultaneously. Wyatt, according to his written testimony, aimed at and hit Frank McLaury in the belly and believed that the second shot came from Billy Clanton, who apparently was aiming at but missed Wyatt. Ike Clanton, who was still unarmed after the court hearing, grabbed Wyatt by the arm—but was pushed aside and thus escaped the melee. One Billy Claiborne, another Cowboy who was unarmed and had been chatting with Ike, fled into Fly's studio and missed the fight altogether. After the first two shots, the fight became general. Tom and Frank McLaury were both killed, as was Billy Clanton. Virgil and Morgan Earp both were seriously wounded, and Doc—hit in the holster—was bruised. Wyatt emerged unscathed. Wyatt and Doc were arrested for murder but were never indicted.

**WHAT IT MEANT**

Popularly known as the gunfight at the OK Corral, the 30-second incident became one of the most well-known stories in the history of the American frontier. It was first popularized in a book called *Wyatt Earp: Frontier Marshal*, written by Stuart Lake and published in 1931. Since then, there have been literally thousands of portrayals of the event, from movies such as *My Darling Clementine* (1946), *Gunfight at the OK Corral* (1957), and *Tombstone* (1993) to television shows such as *Gunsmoke, Broken Arrow,* and *Wyatt Earp.* Although the media at the time and the court transcripts from Cochise County describing the events paint a rather different picture, Wyatt Earp is almost always portrayed and generally regarded as the good guy in the proceedings. This is perhaps because his brother Virgil was later shot and maimed and his brother Morgan was shot and killed by the Cowboys. Wyatt's vendetta became the stuff of legend.

**SALES LESSON**

All very interesting, of course, but how does this relate to sales? Before consultative selling became fashionable, it was widely believed and widely taught that objections were a good thing—they proved interest and even skin in the game. Salespeople were taught to applaud objections and handle them with aplomb. As it turns out, that was poor judgment and bad policy. Truly great selling in fact *prevents* objections in the first place so that there is nothing to handle.

*Preventing objections is better than handling objections.*

Had the Cowboys been treated differently from the beginning of the conflict—had Ike been treated with respectful disagreement rather than angry contempt and accusation—things might have turned out very differently. He might not have armed himself in the first place that crisp October morning in Tombstone if he didn't either (1) seek bloody retribution or (2) fear for his life, or (3) a little of both. Had he not been buffaloed and taken to court by Virgil, cooler heads might have prevailed. The whole shootout was the culmination of what seems to have been a series of misunderstandings, miscalculations, and *mishandling* of the objectionable gun-toting by the Cowboys.

So how does one go about preventing objections? The answer harks back to our discussion of Fabian strategy: (1) Use SPIN questions to develop strong needs, and (2) build sufficient value.

First, do not talk about solutions before you've asked enough questions to develop strong needs. This almost always will degenerate into a conversation about features and advantages, both of which are negatively correlated with sales success. Remember that if you pitch too early, you are likely to lose too often. It is clear that selling features too early is an ineffective and counterproductive selling technique.

When a salesperson is in front of a customer, he or she must resist the temptation to try and "wow" the customer with those cool features that he or she has been told will sell the product. Instead, the salesperson must be disciplined in his or her approach and above all patient. While it is probably true that a good many salespeople are not noted for having the patience of Job, it is nevertheless often one of the key differentiators between average and excellent salespeople. It is ever so important to focus on digging into the customer's business drivers and then mapping the benefits of the solution to those explicit business drivers.

Second, do not talk about solutions until enough value has been created—too often this will lead to price objections. When most of the objections raised reflect doubt about the *value* of the offering, it is most likely that needs have not been developed strongly enough. And certainly not enough value has been created. The answer when these objections are raised is not to handle the objections but to go back and do a better job of needs development. The answer is to go back and create value.

Of course, there will always be some objections, particularly when the product or service being sold does not meet the needs or specifications of the customer exactly. There is always the possibility of a genuine mismatch.

But it is possible to prevent *unnecessary* objections. Unnecessary objections tend to arise as a symptom of poor selling. Less than stellar selling generally will produce lots of objections, which then encourages the inexperienced seller to employ the classic objection-handling techniques of acknowledging, rephrasing, and answering. This is a downward spiral.

Let's look at Figure 10.1 for a moment at the difference between handling objections and preventing objections through the lens of the SPIN model:

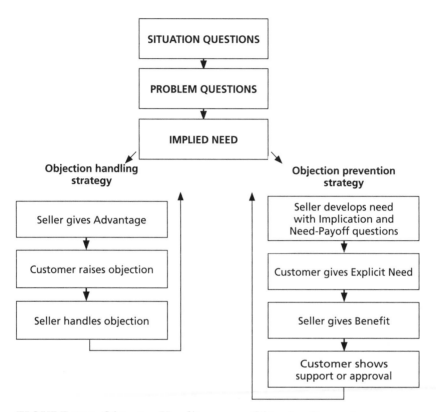

**FIGURE 10.1  Objection Handling versus Objection Prevention**

As you can see, getting the explicit need on the table is the key to preventing objections because it allows the seller to present the all-important benefit rather than the sometimes damaging advantage, which so often raises objections.

Remember that whenever you feel yourself about to pitch, ask yourself, "Is what I am about to say driven by my own impatience or the client's explicit need?" If it is the former, stop yourself and instead ask some better questions.

It is all about the basics. There is no great secret, no new techniques, but rather as Neil Rackham likes to say, "Good selling is good selling." *Aequam memento rebus in arduis servare mentem.*

# 11

## PICKETT'S CHARGE—
## BATTLE OF GETTYSBURG
## U.S. CIVIL WAR (1863)

### ON THROWING GOOD RESOURCES AFTER BAD

*Well, it is all over now. The battle is lost, and many of us are prisoners, many are dead, many wounded, bleeding and dying. Your Soldier lives and mourns and but for you, my darling, he would rather, a million times rather, be back there with his dead, to sleep for all time in an unknown grave.*
—MAJOR GENERAL GEORGE PICKETT, CONFEDERATE STATES
OF AMERICA, TO HIS FIANCÉE, JULY 4, 1863

Pickett's Charge was an infantry assault ordered by Confederate General Robert E. Lee against the center of the Union line on Cemetery Ridge on the last day of the Battle of Gettysburg. Confederate attacks on both Union flanks had failed, and Lee was determined to break through the lines at almost any cost. A lot was riding on a victory in the north. The farthest point reached by the attack is generally regarded as "the high-water mark of the Confederacy." In hindsight (as General Longstreet correctly predicted), Lee should have cut his losses and retreated after the second day. The South never really recovered psychologically from that defeat. *Aut vincere, aut mori.*

The lesson is that it is vital to the health of an organization that you know when to cut your losses on a big deal that is unlikely to be won. It is no good throwing time and money at an account if it is quite simply too costly. Even if you win, it may be a Pyrrhic victory.

**WHAT HAPPENED**

In the earliest hours of July 3, 1863, having failed to flank the Union Army on the previous afternoon and evening (on the second day of fighting at Gettysburg), General Robert E. Lee made plans for a full frontal assault on the Union lines the next morning. Lieutenant General Longstreet, who was to command the charge, strenuously protested the plan. He regarded the battle as already lost. Years later, "Old Pete's" widow, Helen D. Longstreet, quoted Union General Daniel Sickles as saying, "Longstreet told General Lee that there were no fifteen thousand men ever born who could make that march and pierce our centre; nevertheless, General Lee ordered the charge to be made."

It was a sunny, hot (87°F), and humid day. No order had been given to General Pickett to have his men ready to charge at daybreak—so they weren't ready at daybreak. The assault was further delayed by a two-hour artillery barrage to try to take out the Union guns and soften up the Union lines. It accomplished neither. Things were already not looking good when Pickett's men emerged from Spangler's Wood on Seminary Ridge.

Some 12,500 men in nine infantry brigades began that desperate gamble (as Faulkner called it), a three-quarter-mile march over open ground toward the Union guns and massed infantry at the aptly named Cemetery Ridge. The assault could only be described as a *charge* in the broadest sense. In fact, "a hundred cannons of the Federals hurled a rain of canister, grape, and shell down upon Pickett's columns marching gallantly to death over the Pennsylvania valley . . ." (a letter from Union General Daniel Sickles to Helen D. Longstreet).

The men marched in rank, the line almost a mile long, until the last 50 yards, where they broke into a charge of sorts. A group of Confederates made it over the small stone wall that was protecting many of the Union rifles, breaching the lines near the center, only to find that they had nowhere to go. After fierce hand-to-hand combat, with no reinforcements arriving, these brave men were either captured or cut down. That fight is often regarded as "the high-water mark of the Confederacy.

Pickett lost nearly half his division—over 3,000 men. On returning to Seminary Ridge, General Lee ordered him to prepare against a counterattack. Pickett's somber reply: "General Lee, I have no Division now." In all, nearly 7,000 Confederates were killed, wounded, or captured on that fateful day.

As afternoon turned to dusk, General Meade—who had been in command of the Union Army of the Potomac for only six days—had no stomach for a counterattack, and Lee's Army of Northern Virginia slipped away in the rain the next morning.

**WHAT IT MEANT**

The Confederate loss at the three-day Battle of Gettysburg was the turning point of the Civil War. Robert E. Lee's well-deserved reputation for invincibility was broken at last. The North was overwhelmed with the victory. The South had lost the initiative and was on the defensive for the last two years of the war.

Much was riding on Lee's final incursion into the North. Had he been successful, it is quite likely that England and France would have formally recognized the Confederate States of America. There is reasonable speculation too that they actually may have allied themselves with the South and joined the war. In addition, the psychological blow to the Union cause would have been devastating in the extreme, and Lincoln might have lost his reelection campaign in 1864.

Perhaps the most enduring legacy of Gettysburg is Lincoln's famous "Gettysburg Address," which he delivered at the dedication of the Soldiers' National Cemetery at Gettysburg on November 19, 1863. The address concludes thus:

> It is rather for us to be here dedicated to the great task remaining before us—that from these honored dead we take increased devotion to that cause for which they gave the last full measure of devotion—that we here highly resolve that these dead shall not have died in vain—that this nation, under God, shall have a new birth of freedom—and that government of the people, by the people, for the people, shall not perish from the earth.

**SALES LESSON**

The lesson we learn from the third day at Gettysburg is this: There often comes a time to cut your losses and bow out gracefully from the field. The thought is brilliantly depicted in the movie *Tin Cup* when Kevin Costner's title character takes a series of brave and foolish golf shots over a pond to hole out in 12 on the par 4 eighteenth hole, spoiling any hope of victory through pure bloody-mindedness. Sometimes you have to call it a day and say "When." Sometimes you have to recognize that throwing good resources after bad is simply wrong-headedness and bad policy.

*The savvy salesperson knows when to say "when."*

There are times when the wise policy is simply to walk away from a sale. It's hard to do. Sometimes it is the hardest thing in sales to do. It is particularly galling when you have already spent a lot of time, effort, and money working on the sale. You may have made special efforts to see the customer. You actually may have flown out to see the customer face-to-face. Twice! You may have spent hours preparing for and planning sales calls. You may have spent more hours building presentations and proposals. You may have brought your technical people in; you even may have brought your manager into the process. The revenue is forecast. How could you possibly just walk away from the business?

The first thing to understand is the changing nature of customers. Customer expectations have changed. Customers are both more gun-shy and more demanding. They are more gun-shy because of budgetary restraints and a higher degree of oversight. They are more demanding because they can be. They can treat sellers as commodities because they have so many options for any particular solution. Moreover, prospects have begun acting like customers long before they sign on the dotted line. They want meetings, demonstrations, access to your experts, and so many other requests once reserved for paying customers. And if you don't give it to them, someone else will. This is one of the reasons why the pursuit of opportunities costs so much more and why you need to be so much more strategic in deciding which opportunities to pursue. For some organizations, opportunity selection has become a Six Sigma process.

Because of this new paradigm, the salesperson to some degree does have to play the game by the new rules, and this makes it ever more important to make choices and spend money wisely. Once you've made the decision to pursue an account, you tend to go all-in. Correctly. The question is how do you know when the sale is not going to close? How do you know when to pull the plug? As I said in Chapter 2 on planning, there are four possible outcomes of a sales call in the complex sale: the *advance* or the *order* (both of which are positive outcomes) and the *continuation* or the *no sale* (both of which are negative outcomes).

When you encounter a no-sale situation, it should be an easy decision to pull the plug. Recall that no sale is a clear indication from the customer that the sales cycle will not continue. It occurs when the salesperson is shut down with a definitive, "No, we will not do business with you." Unfortunately, it's a hard message to hear. And if an enormous amount of effort has already gone into the sale, it is tempting to simply ignore it and carry on as though the sale were still alive. Do not succumb to this temptation. Bow out gracefully. You never know when the customer's current choice may fail, and he or she will come crawling back to you. Keep the lines of communication open, and do not be a sore loser.

The more difficult decision is to pull the plug when the customer has *not* shut the sale down definitively. This occurs when the customer continues to show an interest—even a lively interest in your products or services—but makes no commitment that advances the sale. How do you know when to walk away then? This is the crux of the matter. How many continuations do you accept in the sales process before you know for certain that the sale will never close? This is a difficult question. And unfortunately, it is not an exact science. You may have to be willing to go with your gut sometimes.

The first thing is to *ask* the customer for a commitment that demonstrates a willingness to put at least some skin in the game. Just flat out ask for what you want. Ask for a meeting with the boss, for example. Ask the customer to take some *action* that shows he or she is at least willing to try to make the sale work. If you don't ask, it is unlikely that the customer will offer to do anything of his or her own accord. Why should he or she?

The second thing is to be willing to walk away if the customer refuses to take any action on behalf of moving the sale forward. You have to be genuinely willing to cut your losses. You cannot bluff. This is not a poker game. It is in neither of your best interests to approach a sale as though it is a game of skill or chance. A sale ought never pit the salesperson against the customer in an adversarial, zero-sum situation. Commerce—the trafficking of goods and services—is about both a buyer and a seller being better off by virtue of what one gave and what the other got. A sale is an exchange for *mutual benefit*. If the customer is unwilling to see the sale in those terms, he or she is not ultimately a customer you want to do business with. Such a customer will bleed you dry, and you will walk away with nothing. As crooner Kenny Rogers put it so well in his lovely song, "The Gambler": "Know when to walk away; know when to run."

# PART 2

## ACCOUNT STRATEGY

# 12

## GREAT SWAMP FIGHT—KING PHILIP'S WAR NEW ENGLAND COLONIES VERSUS NARRAGANSETT TRIBE (1675)

### ENTRY STRATEGY: ON USING THE FOCUS OF DISSATISFACTION

*Fences work and the walls work and separations work.*
*They afford to any nation the delay of entry.*
—CONGRESSMAN DUNCAN HUNTER

During one of the coldest weeks on record in New England in December of 1675, the colonists of Massachusetts Bay, Plymouth Colony, and Connecticut joined forces to attack the neutral Narragansett Indian tribe in Rhode Island. King Philip's War had been raging (between the English colonists and the Wampanoag Confederacy) for several months, and Governor Winslow of Plymouth decided that a preemptive strike on the Narragansetts would not be unwarranted. Some 3,000 Narragansett warriors had gathered with their women and children in a hidden fort in the Great Swamp of Rhode Island. The fort was well-nigh impregnable under normal conditions, but this particular winter was so cold that the swamp had frozen over—allowing easy access. A captured Indian named Peter was willing to turn coat because he had had a falling out with one of the Narragansett sachems. He led the colonial fighting men to the fort in the Great Swamp. After long and brutal fighting, the English colonists burned the fort to the ground.

The sales lesson from this story is about the importance of finding a focus of dissatisfaction, one of three types of sponsors for penetrating an account.

**WHAT HAPPENED**

King Philip's War was by proportion of population the bloodiest war in American history. Enormous casualties were inflicted, and horrendous atrocities were committed—on both sides. Unrest between the Wampanoag Indians and the New England Colonies had been brewing for some years, chiefly over colonial westward expansion and Puritan highhandedness in dealing with the Native American.

Hostilities escalated into all-out war in 1675 after three Wampanoags were hanged for the murder of one John Sassamon, a counselor to King Philip who had turned traitor. It seems that he had told the authorities at Plymouth Colony that the Wampanoag chief was preparing for war. Outraged Wampanoag warriors began terrorizing the settlers at Swansea, and the United Colonies of New England—which included Connecticut, Massachussetts, and Plymouth—responded in force. A very bloody and very costly war had begun.

The powerful Narragansett tribe, which lived mostly in Rhode Island (which was not part of the colonial confederacy), had managed a policy of neutrality in the proceedings but had begun sheltering Wampanoag women and children. The United Colonies' alliance, which actually had been formed back in 1643 partly in response to the supposed Narragansett threat, decided to take a hard line. They enticed the Narragansetts into a treaty that included a provision that they would give up any Wampanoags that were found on their lands. Whether they had ever planned to abide by this treaty is in question. Regardless, they ignored the provision and continued looking after Wampanoag women and children.

In late October, the United Colonies asked the Narragansetts for reassurances that the treaty was still in force. Really, it was more of an ultimatum to comply with the terms agreed on. This time the Narragansetts flatly refused. The United Colonies decided to send an expedition to Narragansett territory to force the issue. Noncompliance in the face of an army would be grounds for a preemptive strike.

The United Colonies raised the largest army yet gathered in New England to prepare for possible assault. One thousand soldiers, including 150 Mohegan Indians, under the command of Plymouth Governor Josiah Winslow began assembling at Wickford, a harbor town in the Colony of Rhode Island, which was chosen as the staging area. Operations were to begin in early December. Rhode Island agreed to help out with the massive logistics problem of looking after an army of that size in the cold New England winter.

Scouting parties around Wickford managed to capture several Narragansetts. One of the captured warriors, who was known as Peter, turned out to be somewhat disaffected, and in the end, he betrayed his tribe. He told the colonists that the Nararagansetts were hiding Wampanoags in a secluded fort in the nearby swamp. He even went so far as to agree to serve as guide to the camp. Governor Winslow, who was facing a logistical nightmare, decided to set out immediately. In the early morning of December 19, 1675, the expedition set out for the Great Swamp in blinding snow and near-record cold. By afternoon, Peter had led the army more than 15 miles to the fortified village.

The Narragansett fort was indeed formidable. It was surrounded by water and a high wooden palisade, which, as it turned out, was not quite finished. The colonists attacked single file across a log causeway and were twice repulsed by heavy fire and brutal fighting before finally managing to break through the defenses. They entered the fort, where fighting became desperate in and around the hundreds of wigwams that were full of women and children. In the end, the colonists set fire to the wigwams. By late afternoon, it was a clear loss for the Narragansetts, many of whom fled into the swamp.

So ended the Great Swamp Fight. Winslow's army marched the entire way back to Wickford that night in the ice and snow, carrying their wounded. They had won a decisive victory but at a terrible cost. Winslow had lost over 200 men, dead or wounded. The Narragansetts had lost as many as 600—at least half of which were women and children. *Deserta faciunt et pacem appellant.*

**WHAT IT MEANT**

The Great Swamp Fight took a great toll on the Narragansetts—not least because a large part of their winter food supply was put to the torch. But the battle ensured their joining the war against the colonists, which raged on until August of 1676, when King Philip was finally killed, beheaded, and quartered.

King Philip's War nearly destroyed the Massachusetts Colony and very nearly annihilated the Wampanoag and Narragansett tribes in New England. As many as 6,000 Native Americans were either killed or captured, and many were sold into slavery. Somewhere around 2,500 English settlers—men, women, and children—died during the war.

Perhaps most damaging to the colonies was the financial burden the war had laid on the backs of the settlers. The war cost an estimated 100,000 pounds sterling. Back in England, investors were not pleased. Rather than paying off handsomely, their colonial investments had ended up costing immense sums of money. The British government began to take a more active role in colonial affairs.

**SALES LESSON**

The Great Swamp Fight teaches us about the value of finding the *focus of dissatisfaction* in an account and using that person in the account-penetration strategy. Had the captive Peter been unwilling to betray his companions and provide guidance to the colonists, Winslow may never have found the Narragansett stronghold. Things may have turned out much differently.

Successful salespeople create an entry strategy that gets them to the decision maker in the most efficient and economical way possible. It is usually done with the use of a sponsor—someone inside the company (account) who can guide, direct, advise, and introduce the salesperson around, even perhaps representing his or her interests within the company. Sometimes, instead of relying on an individual sponsor, successful salespeople may seek out a focus within the account—perhaps a person but also perhaps a committee or even a department—that can help them get started in the company. In an especially complex sale, it would not be surprising to find a successful salesperson using several different sponsors, or focus points, to assist him or her in gaining entry.

There are three specific focus points where salespeople need to look for sponsors:

- *The focus of receptivity*—the point in an account where receptive people who are prepared to listen sympathetically are located
- *The focus of dissatisfaction*—the point in an account where people are unhappy with the current system or supplier
- *The focus of power*—the elusive point in an account where the person or people who are actually able to make the decision are located

It is generally easiest when preparing an entry strategy to look for a focus of receptivity—someone from whom you can find out information about the account and the people in it and through whom you can gain access to a focus of dissatisfaction. The important thing is not to try to impress the focus of receptivity as though he or she could make the decision. This will just bog the sale down. It is important to get to the people who have a problem that you can solve as expeditiously as possible.

The reason for this is that without dissatisfaction, there is simply no basis for a sale. A person who is completely satisfied with the status quo doesn't need you. It behooves the salesperson to think of his or her product or service as the solution to a problem. If there is no problem to solve, then there will be no sale. Any success will be possible only if the salesperson can identify a person, group, or function that is hurting in an area in which he or she can make a difference.

For the successful salesperson, finding the focus of dissatisfaction is the key to the entry strategy. Once that person or function is identified, the great thing is to get to him or her, usually with the help of the focus of receptivity. Once in, there are two strategic objectives for the sales call with the focus of dissatisfaction. These objectives are to

1. Uncover the problem and develop it to the point where the customer decides that he or she must take action.
2. Use the trouble point that's been developed into an explicit need to get access to the decision maker.

Remember, the focus of dissatisfaction can be a great champion—but in a complex sale, that person is rarely the decision maker. It's no good selling the focus of dissatisfaction on the need for your product or service if he or she can't or won't take the problem and solution to the higher echelons where the decision to buy can be made. Ideally, he or she will provide access to the decision maker. But if he or she is unwilling or unable to get the salesperson in front of the focus of power, the next step is to groom this focus of dissatisfaction to do the internal selling for you. One way or another, it is crucial that the explicit need gets in front of the decision maker in such a way that he or she will be compelled to act.

Governor Winslow used the disgruntled Narragansett Peter (who might perhaps be called a focus of dissatisfaction) to guide him through the swamp and get him access to the fort. Chapter 13 will look at the importance of the focus of power.

# 13

## BATTLE OF AUGHRIM—WILLIAMITE WAR WILLIAM III VERSUS THE JACOBITES (1691)

### ENTRY STRATEGY: ON GAINING ACCESS TO THE FOCUS OF POWER

*Anybody can win—unless there happens to be a second entry.*
—GEORGE ADE

The Battle of Aughrim was the last important battle of the Williamite War in Ireland. The Jacobites, by now under the command of Charles Chalmont, carefully chose the battlefield near the village of Aughrim in County Galway. What appeared to be a limestone plain was in point of fact a limestone slab protected in front by a vast bog. On the fateful, misty morning of July 12, 1691, a large part of the Williamite main force, led by Godert de Ginkel (after King William III had returned to England), marched unawares into the bog and were cut down. All appeared to be lost until the Williamites found a path to the limestone slab. General mayhem was visited on the now-trapped Jacobites. More than 7,000 people were killed that day—more than any other day in Irish history.

The sales lesson is about gaining access to the decision maker. Use the dissatisfaction that you've developed in the recognition of needs stage as a means for gaining access to the decision maker—to get to the focus of power.

**WHAT HAPPENED**

The Battle of Aughrim was the decisive battle of the Williamite War fought between the Catholic supporters of the deposed King James II and the armies of Protestant King William III (of Orange and William and Mary fame). William had supplanted James II as King of England, Scotland, and Ireland in the Glorious Revolution of 1688. The Irish, three-fourths of whom were Catholic, had appreciated the religious tolerance of James and did not appreciate the overthrow.

In the second Jacobite uprising (from the Latin name Jacobus—meaning James—Jacobite refers to those who would raise James to the throne), Richard Talbot, 1st Earl of Tyrconnell and Lord Deputy of Ireland, conquered all the fortified places in Ireland (except Derry) on James' behalf. The deposed king himself arrived in Ireland with 6,000 French troops to try to regain his throne but fled again after being thrashed at the Battle of the Boyne in 1690.

After the Boyne, French General Charles Chalmont, Marquis de Saint-Ruth, took over command of the Irish/French Jacobite forces. Although counseled against giving battle, Chalmont chose the town of

Aughrim to make a stand against the Williamite forces under Dutch General Godert de Ginkel. The Williamite forces were composed of troops from 10 nationalities, most notably Dutch, Scottish, British, Danish, and French Huguenots. Ironically, the Protestant William was supported by the Pope. His elite Dutch Blue Guard carried the papal banner.

The choice of ground was brilliant and was used to every advantage. The defense was centered on the hill of Kilcommedon, which rose gradually behind a morass. The ruins of the Castle of Aughrim were at the north end, approached by a narrow causeway between two bogs. The pass of Urrachree, guarded by sand dunes, lay to the south.

Unfortunately, Chalmont had refused to share his battle plan with his subordinates—especially Patrick Sarsfield, who held him responsible for the loss of Athlone two weeks earlier. Sarsfield's cavalry was relegated to a reserve position behind the right flank. When Chalmont was decapitated by a cannonball, the end was in sight.

The battle was fought gallantly on both sides, but in the end, the Williamites prevailed. After much attack and counterattack and a great deal of spilled blood, Ginkel finally ordered a cavalry charge across the causeway to the castle and village. The defenders then discovered, to their horror, that their reserve ammunition—which was made in Britain—did not fit into their French rifles. The day was lost.

**WHAT IT MEANT**

The Battle of Aughrim effectively ended Jacobite hopes for restoration of the Stuart monarchy. Shortly thereafter, Galway surrendered without a fight, as did Limerick after a short siege. The Treaty of Limerick allowed the remainder of the Jacobite army, under the command of Patrick Sarsfield, to leave for service in the French Army. The exodus to France is known as the "Flight of the Wild Geese."

**SALES LESSON**

The lesson for sales has to do with gaining access to the person or function in a company (account) that wields purchasing authority and what to do when you get there. In Chapter 12, you learned to concentrate on the focus of dissatisfaction. Now let's turn to the *focus of power*.

There are three questions that may be worth exploring briefly:

- How do you identify *when* a senior executive will be most receptive to your request for time?
- What is the most effective route to obtain an audience with a C-level executive (CLE)?
- How do you execute the meeting with the CLE in order to increase your chances for success?

First, what is the optimal time to gain an audience with a CLE? Unlike commodity-driven purchasing agents, CLEs rarely get up in the morning thinking about interacting with salespeople. So what *do* they think about? They are hyperfocused on improving their results and employing strategies that will help their enterprise grow revenue, increase market share, counter a competitive threat, acquire new customers, increase customer loyalty and retention, bolster margins, decrease costs, manage risk, increase shareholder value, attract and retain skilled staff, and improve workforce productivity. CLEs employ a huge variety of strategies to improve in these areas.

One thing is certain: If you can't clearly prove that what you are selling will help an executive improve in at least one of these areas, then you need not waste your time calling on the C-suite. The occupants don't want to see you. However, if you can show that your offering will enhance results in these key strategic areas, you are still in the game.

The maxim "Timing is everything" is massively relevant to those in the sales profession. If you know when CLEs are likely to be engaged in making a major purchase decision, then your odds of being "at the right place at the right time" will increase dramatically. You must find out where they are in the buying cycle.

Once you have cultivated the *focus of dissatisfaction* (FOD), how do you succeed in leveraging that relationship to gain access to the C-suite? The model for getting time with a CLE requires two key steps. First, you must create the willingness for your contact, the FOD, to see the strategic value of providing access to the boss. You must remember that this access is closely guarded and that entry is provided to only a select few. In essence, you must build trust with every interaction and prove that the meeting will be valuable and a good use of precious CLE time.

To accomplish this goal, you have to invest time and resources to expand the FOD's understanding of his or her company's challenges and desired state. There are several methods you may employ, including interviews, diagnostic tools, focus groups, needs assessments, and so on. The key element is that you need to make your FOD look good in the eyes of his or her boss and be prepared to shed new insights on the company's strategy, opportunities, and challenges. Be certain that there is some level of equanimity in the relationship. Your FOD also should invest time and provide access during this phase of the buying process.

Next, you must be able to clearly state the value and outcomes of a meeting with your FOD and the CLE. Be certain that you rehearse this request long before making the actual inquiry. The value of this meeting must be crystal clear to your FOD because you want him or her to make the request. Your chance of securing a meeting with a CLE increases exponentially when it is made by a trusted direct report.

Finally, you must be relentless and focused in order to build the trust and strategic value necessary to gain and maintain access to the CLE. There are three key reasons that your access to a CLE may be blocked:

1. *Your sponsoring FOD is not held in high regard by the CLE.* If this is the case, you have only one choice. You must find another FOD who has right level of respect and influence and can get you access to the CLE.
2. *The buyer has moved beyond recognition of needs to evaluation of options.* In this case, your access will be blocked until the point of choosing a final vendor is imminent. C-level executives aren't in the business of vetting potential suppliers. This is the domain of their employees. If you find yourself in this unenviable yet very real situation, your strategy must be to differentiate at a level that allows you to make it to the finalist round in the selection process. At this juncture, the CLE most likely will reinsert himself or herself in the decision process.
3. *Your sponsor doesn't trust you.* Now, it is very rare indeed that you will ever receive this feedback directly. You can bet that if (a) your

prospect is in recognition of needs and (b) your sponsor has a positive relationship with the CLE and you are not granted access, lack of trust is the real reason for this blockage. If this is the case, you will get a litany of excuses that are nothing more than smokescreens. At this point you must completely overhaul your strategy and determine how to provide new strategic value and insight to your FOD.

Now that I've covered when and how to reach a CLE, let's explore what you *must* do when meeting with a CLE that will increase your chances of success dramatically and keep the door open in the future.

The CLE call is unlike any other call you make, and you must be prepared at a level that goes far beyond ordinary call planning. Here is the critical knowledge you must have in advance of this meeting and some of the sources that provide this information:

| Knowledge | Sources |
|---|---|
| Overall business strategy<br><br>Potential problems and opportunities | *Information:* 10K, analyst reports, analyst conference calls, Web-based intelligence sources (Hoover's, Lexis-Nexis, First Research, etc.)<br><br>*People:* Focus of receptivity, focus of dissatisfaction, competitors |
| Understanding of the most urgent problems/opportunities facing the CLE's business | *People:* Focus of dissatisfaction |
| Implications of not solving problems or maximizing opportunities | |
| The payoffs/outcomes from fixing problems and/or maximizing opportunities | |

If you do not have a clear and concise understanding of the information listed in this table, then you are not ready for a meeting with a CLE. Some experienced sales professionals may be a bit alarmed at this point and wonder why you would ever want to engage in a dialogue with CLE's direct reports first. Wouldn't they just try to block access to the CLE? The simple answer is no, with a caveat. If the CLE's direct reports are strategic and talented, then they will not block you. If they aren't strategic and talented, then you may not want to do business with this executive anyway. Since a CLE is rarely, if ever, intimately involved in the implementation of any solution, you will have to rely on his or her direct reports for a successful implementation. If they are not talented and capable, you are in trouble. It is better to know this information sooner rather than later.

Alright, you're invited to meet with the CLE and three vice presidents next week. Is there a successful road map and agenda for this type of meeting? Yes, always. In the first three minutes of the meeting, you must impress everyone in the room, especially the CLE, or it's over. A solid, strategic agenda delivered with poise and confidence will ensure that you get off to a smashing start. Here is the agenda you should follow for a meeting when a CLE is in the recognition of needs phase of the buying cycle:

- Business issues facing the company
- Challenges/opportunities
- Your diagnosis/insight
- Capabilities to drive improvement
- Solution components/expertise
- Next steps

The execution of this meeting is extraordinarily critical. Your focus of dissatisfaction should coach you on the development of key talking points, but such talking points can't let you move significantly from the agenda just laid out. CLE's in recognition of needs want you to prove that you

- Have done your homework
- Know the problems/opportunities facing their company
- Know the problems/opportunities facing their area/operation

- Can reveal something that he or she didn't know about the business (in a nonthreatening manner)
- Have the capabilities to help the CLE execute his or her strategy
- Have done this before and are capable of doing it again

Success depends on your ability to engage the CLE in a dialogue and gain additional insight and perspective that is resident only with and closely guarded by the CLE. Why do I say *closely guarded?* CLEs like to discuss success, results, and strategy to drive more of the same. They do not like to discuss problems, implications, and potential failure. If you arrive at this meeting ready to dig in and develop pain when this information is available through other sources, then you most certainly will not be asked to come back. However, if you arrive and already know the problems and opportunities and the resulting impact of not changing, then you are in absolutely outstanding shape and undoubtedly far ahead of your competition. It is in this portion of the call that you highlight your knowledge of your prospect's problems/opportunities and hopefully can reveal something new or shed a new light on something with which the CLE is familiar.

Your mission now is to ask the CLE to react to your diagnosis of the business—to affirm or refute the problems/challenges that he or she faces and expand on the impact of those problems/challenges. If you gain agreement in this area and more than one problem/challenge exists, then you must ask the CLE to rank them in order of importance.

At this point, the CLE is confident that you know the business, you have developed a thorough understanding of the implications of not making any changes, and you have provided a nonthreatening platform for the CLE to react to your diagnosis and add his or her extremely valuable perspective. Now you arrive at another critical juncture.

The next step in the meeting is to ask the CLE to describe the payoff and improvements he or she expects from fixing these problems and/or maximizing opportunities. The goal of these questions is to get the CLE to describe what improvement will do for his or her strategy and business. Always plan these questions in advance, and be certain that they sound informed, positive, and natural.

After you have uncovered the payoffs that the CLE would expect from addressing a problem/opportunity, the next step is to provide a brief overview describing your capabilities and how they would help the CLE attain his or her desired state. The goal is not to deliver a detailed proposal but to provide enough detail to

- Demonstrate that you have the capabilities to help the CLE address a problem/opportunity and more effectively execute his or her strategy
- Get some high-level feedback from the CLE that helps you to develop and shape your solution proposal/presentation

If you cover this much ground in your meeting, consider yourself the epitome of professionalism and success. The next question you need to ask relates to the process the company will follow in making a major purchase decision. The best way to posit this question is to be brief, direct, and customer-focused. For example, you might ask, "In order to be sure that I'm working with your team in the most effective manner, would you please advise me on the process you normally follow when making strategic purchase decisions such as this one?" The key is to get the CLE talking, which allows you to ask additional questions so that you obtain a clear understanding of the process.

Once you know the process, then the next and final step for this meeting is to understand how the prospect organization will go about the task of making a choice between competing vendors. In essence, you need to understand which differentiators will inform and guide the prospect's decision process. These differentiators, or *decision criteria*, will provide the insight necessary to lead your sales campaign to a successful conclusion.

This critical step is almost always ignored, even by some very experienced sellers. If you sell an offering that is not a routine purchase, then your buyer most likely doesn't have the requisite experience to make an intelligent, informed decision. In fact, you can be assured that the CLE and his or her team are quite concerned that they will make the wrong decision owing to incorrect or incomplete criteria.

If time doesn't allow you to cover this critical topic with the CLE, then be certain to gather as much of this information as possible from the CLE's direct reports after the meeting and prepare to confirm and build on what you've learned in the next meeting with the CLE.

Selling in the C-suite is the most coveted of all selling opportunities. Understand that if you take the steps outlined in this chapter, your chances for success at the C-level improve dramatically. But there is no silver bullet. You must work hard and follow a process. *Cura omnia potest.*

# 14

## THE BUYING CYCLE: IMPLEMENTATION
## (ON THE IMPORTANCE OF FOLLOW-UP)

*Those people blessed with the most talent don't necessarily outperform everyone else.*
*It's the people with follow-through who excel.*
—MARY KAY ASH

The reign of Pharaoh (Queen) Hatshepsut, "foremost of noble ladies," was one of many bright spots in Egyptian history. She was the fifth pharaoh of the fabulous Eighteenth Egyptian Dynasty. There is no record of war in her time. It was a time of peace and development of all that is noble in the human psyche. For the last seven years of her reign, she was coregent with her nephew/stepson Thutmose III. Cities as far as Tyre and Sidon in Syria paid tribute, and all was at rest and prosperous. Those were the salad days of the dynasty.

On the death of Hatshepsut, usually dated to 1458 BC, a coalition of Canaanites revolted against Egyptian hegemony. They were joined by the Kingdom of Mitanni—which stretched from southeast Anatolia (modern Turkey) and northern Syria to the banks of the Euphrates. As was common in ancient times (and indeed is often the case in the corporate world today), the natives grew restless with a change in leadership and often rebelled to test the mettle of the new pharaoh.

Pharaoh Thutmose III, now 21 years old, was no pushover. A brilliant strategist and an accomplished horseman and archer, Thutmose III was the man for the crisis. In fact, as it turned out, Thutmose III— sometimes called the "Napoleon of Egypt"—was one of the few generals in history who never lost a battle. This makes the comparison with Napoleon not exactly an apt one.

**WHAT HAPPENED**

Thutmose quickly gathered his forces and marched them north to deal with the insurrection, which was led by the King of Kadesh. On reaching Aruna, south of Megiddo, Thutmose rested his army. He had a choice to make and took counsel with all his generals. The rebels had gathered their army at the walled city of Megiddo, and there were three possible routes of advance to meet them. A range of mountains rising at Mount Carmel and stretching inland stood between the Egyptian army and the confederation.

The northern or southern routes were preferred by the Egyptian general staff because they were much less taxing, and the generals had what turned out to be false intelligence that the central route was guarded by the Canaanites. And anyway, the central pass was a much more difficult journey for an army. They counseled Thutmose to take one of the easier routes, but Thutmose was as adamant as he was brave. As the beloved Son of Ra (the Sun god), he reckoned that all would be well if he took the narrow road. All was in fact well, and the vanguard of his army reached the Jezreel Valley at Megiddo unmolested in only 12 hours. The last troops emerged from the pass seven hours later, watched over by Thutmose himself. He rested his army for the night and in the morning deployed them in three separate wings—behind the enemy.

Thutmose had caught the enemy completely unawares because they had expected and prepared for Thutmose to take one of the other two routes. On discovering the huge Egyptian army now in their rear, the confederates had to quickly redeploy their troops, most of whom panicked and fled to the city walls, leaving their horses and chariots of gold and silver behind in the encampments. It was a complete rout. The young and inexperienced Egyptian soldiers, however, rather than immediately press their advantage, were blinded by the lure of plunder and decided to indulge in some good, old-fashioned looting, much to the chagrin of their valiant leader.

While the Egyptian troops, all wet behind the ears, were busy grabbing everything they could from the abandoned encampments, the city gate was firmly closed, and the last of the rebel soldiers were pulled over the walls into the city. Thutmose was pretty upset at the turn of events as he watched his troops squander the opportunity for a quick and decisive win, and with good reason. There were in fact more than 300 enemy kings represented on the field that day, and as the inscription from the Amen Temple at Karnak puts it, "The capture of Megiddo is the capture of a thousand towns."

The Egyptians, having failed to follow-up the rout in favor of pillaging, were now in the unenviable position of laying siege to a fortified city. Indeed, they ended up having to build a wooden palisade around the city, dig a moat, and let no one pass except those who wanted to surrender. And so a battle that could have been over in a matter of hours turned into a siege that lasted seven months. At last, the defeated kings sued for peace, took oaths of allegiance, paid tribute, and were allowed to return home with the "breath of life" yet in their nostrils.

Tjaneni, private secretary to Thutmose III, recorded the events of the battle and siege, and his story was later engraved on the walls of the Amen Temple at Karnak. In fact, this is the first recorded battle in history. It is also the first *recorded* use of the composite bow (there is archeological evidence of the use of composite bows by nomads of the Asiatic steppes in the fourth century BC) and apparently the first recorded body count from a battle.

The conquest of Megiddo laid the groundwork for the pacification of the Levant and allowed Thutmose III to begin the extension of his empire. Thutmose III fought 17 campaigns (almost one per year for the rest of his reign) and never lost a battle. At its height, his empire stretched from northern Syria and the Euphrates all the way south to the fourth waterfall on the Nile in Nubia. Thutmose's success in some ways can be attributed to him never forgetting the lesson of his first major battle—the importance of quick, decisive follow-up and follow-through. *Difficile est tenere quae acceperis nisi exerceas.*

In sales this lesson holds true as well. The signing of the deal is not the time to celebrate: Wait until after a successful implementation for the celebration, and let the customer lead that celebration. Had the Egyptian army been comprised of disciplined veterans, it would have foregone the plundering until after the absolute victory. As it was, Egypt having had enjoyed a long period of peace, there were no veterans, and the army was made up of new recruits, unskilled in the art of war and drawn to treasure like rats to garbage. By celebrating early, they lost the opportunity to capture the King of Kadesh and all his underlings in one fell swoop. Instead, they were forced to endure the rigors of a long siege in a foreign land.

It is the naive salesperson who uncorks the champagne the moment the deal is signed on the dotted line. Enjoy the bubbly certainly, but prepare for the grueling work ahead *in the new account*, for it is after the contract is signed that the real work begins. It is one of the most common strategic errors that inexperienced (and even some experienced) salespeople make—to assume that the account now can be thrown over the wall to the project managers or other implementation resources as the salesperson happily trots on to new sales.

Working closely with the customer during what is called the *implementation phase of the buying cycle* is one of the more strategic aspects of selling. For those of you unfamiliar with the buying cycle, Huthwaite's storied research into the behaviors of successful sellers produced a model of the customer decision process. In major sales, buyers—whether influencers, decision makers, purchasing agents, or evaluation committees—progress through discrete phases when they make decisions. By understanding these stages and how to influence them, sellers find it easier to form practical account strategies that move sales forward.

Effective selling begins with an understanding of how people *buy*. All of Huthwaite's sales-improvement initiatives have at their core perspective focus on the buyer—embodied in the buying cycle as shown here in Figure 14.1:

**FIGURE 14.1 The Buying Cycle**

*Changes over time.* The first phase of the buying cycle is that time when prospects are enjoying the status quo and have not yet recognized a need for change, but times are changing. With the ever-increasing velocity of business change and the unpredictable nature of the world of commerce in general, buyers are spending more and more time in this phase as their needs evolve and change in reaction to these rapid and volatile market cycles. Sellers (and their marketing departments) can help to jump-start the buying process by delivering provocative and compelling prospecting messages that help buyers appreciate potential challenges and opportunities.

*Recognition of needs.* During this stage, potential buyers become dissatisfied with their existing situation and begin to realize a need to solve a problem or exploit an opportunity. The role of the seller is to uncover the source of dissatisfaction and increase the buyers' perception of its intensity and urgency.

*Evaluation of options.* Once they've agreed on the need for change, buyers then start considering alternatives for resolving their dissatisfaction. Here the sales professional's job is to help buyers understand how the selling organization can best address their needs. The excellent seller will influence the criteria the customer organization uses to evaluate competing vendors in his or her favor.

*Resolution of concerns.* Next, buyers tentatively select a vendor, but before signing the contract, they will assess any associated risks and consequences. Sellers need to uncover these concerns or fears and help to resolve them.

*Decision.* At this point, the deal is agreed on, and the contract is signed.

*Implementation.* After the sale is made, the customer organization begins to introduce, test, and install the seller's solution. Buyers expect to receive the value promised by the seller and to realize a return on their investment. The seller's responsibility is to help the customer adopt the solution and overcome any implementation challenges.

*Changes over time.* The cycle does not end just because the customer organization is implementing a solution. Inevitably, there will be changes in the account—contacts may turn over, company strategy may change, reorganizations or mergers may occur. Each of these changes offers opportunities for the seller to strengthen the relationship by helping buyers anticipate and address additional problems and opportunities.

I shall revisit the buying cycle on occasion throughout this book.

Let's turn our attention now to the implementation phase of the cycle. Selling is all about alignment with the customer's frame of reference. Abandon the customer in the implementation phase, and you can quickly undo all that effort you put in demonstrating to the customer that you are a partner and not a vendor and be unceremoniously dumped back into the category of "typical salesperson" in the customer's perception of you.

Implementation is an anxious and difficult time psychologically for customers. They begin to have doubts and worries. "Did I choose the right vendor? Is this really going to work? My career's on the line, for goodness' sake!" And these are legitimate doubts and worries. This is the time when the buyer's choice faces the acid test. Results hang in the balance. The salesperson needs to stand with this apprehensive customer every step of the way.

According to our research, customers go through three psychological stages during the implementation of a new product or service. The first is the "new toy" stage, during which users are almost giddy with excitement. Cool new stuff. They are motivated to learn. They try out all its marvelous bells and whistles and interesting features. This is a time of genuine delight with the product: Everything seems to be just brand new and shiny.

But then the learning stage arrives almost on cue. Users must put in all kinds of time and effort to learn the actual functionality and how to obtain real results. This is hard work. And often boring work. And they don't see immediate results. They want instantaneous success and may feel that they've been oversold if they don't get it. This is when the proverbial *motivation dip*, which I shall discuss in Chapter 17, sets in.

Handle the motivation dip successfully, and users move on to the effectiveness stage. This is when users become at least competent in using the new product or service to maximum effect. They are pleased with the product—and if he or she has stuck by them through the hard part, then they are pleased with the seller. Everything turns up roses, and the seller is in a strategic position to cross-sell or up-sell. The seller now rises to that much-sought-after level of trusted advisor.

Now that implementation has been successful—with the seller's constant vigilance and assistance—the customer is on the cusp of changes over time. From the seller's perspective, this is extremely arable ground for account development. This is an active time for the seller to be looking for ways to expand in the new account. He or she can cultivate, grow, and bring forth fruit. And all because he or she followed up quickly and effectively with the customer through a difficult implementation.

Follow-up is the key, which Thutmose III and his troops learned the hard way. Do not make the same mistake that this army of inexperienced soldiers made so many years ago. Do not celebrate too much too soon. Stay the course, be there for the customer, and support the customer even when he or she appears to be unreasonable or overreliant on you. Think about your own buying experiences and how you felt when the salesperson didn't call you back or pushed you off to a service person and left you thinking, "Typical salesperson. Once the deal is done, he or she no longer cares." Do the hard work, stay engaged, and you will find fertile selling ground. Remember that the greater rewards are not in a quick plunder but rather in a long-term mutually beneficial relationship. I shall explore the importance of a successful implementation phase in Chapter 23.

# 15

## CHARGE OF THE LIGHT BRIGADE—
## CRIMEAN WAR
## BRITISH VERSUS THE RUSSIANS (1854)

### THE BUYING CYCLE: IMPLEMENTATION 2
### (ON THE CONSEQUENCES OF
### FAILURE TO ALIGN INTERNALLY)

*"Theirs not to reason why,*
*Theirs but to do and die.*
*Into the valley of Death*
*Rode the six hundred."*
—ALFRED LORD TENNYSON, "CHARGE OF THE LIGHT BRIGADE"

The Charge of the Light Brigade was led by Lord Cardigan against Russian forces during the Battle of Balaclava in the Crimean War. This incredibly brave and tragic charge was the result of poor communication and misalignment of vision by the British leadership. The light cavalry rode into cannon from three sides and was largely destroyed.

The lesson is on the second part of *planning for implementation*: Internal alignment is crucial before attempting to sell a major piece of business. You may sell the business (break through the lines), but you may end up alone in an angry mob with no backup.

**WHAT HAPPENED** The bravest, most reckless, and perhaps most foolhardy cavalry charge in the annals of British warfare took place on October 25, 1854, during the Battle of Balaclava in the Crimean War. It was for all its glory and magnificence directed at the wrong target.

Lord Raglan, commander of the British Army in the Crimea, ordered the charge from the Sapouné Ridge overlooking the "valley of death" from the western heights. The Light Brigade of the British Cavalry, consisting of the 4th and 13th Light Dragoons, 17th Lancers, and the 8th and 11th Hussars, under the command of Major General James Brudenell, the 7th Earl of Cardigan, were grouped in the valley 600 feet below. To the left of the North Valley, from Lord Raglan's position, were the Fedioukine Hills, where 14 Russian cannons were ensconced. To the right, the south side of the valley was bordered by the Causeway Heights, where 11 Russian battalions had recently dislodged the Turks and now had 32 guns commanding the valley. Straight ahead, a bit over a mile down the narrow valley, the main body of the Russian Cavalry was positioned behind 12 guns.

Lord Raglan sent Captain Louis Edward Nolan with a written order for Lieutenant General George Bingham, 3rd Earl of Lucan, Lord Cardigan's brother-in-law and nemesis, who had overall command of the Light and Heavy Brigades of the Cavalry. The order was somewhat vague: "Lord Raglan wishes the Cavalry to advance rapidly to the front, follow the enemy, and try to prevent the enemy carrying away the guns. Troop Horse Artillery may accompany. French Cavalry is on your left.

Immediate." Lord Lucan, who was down in the valley, could not see the redoubts that had been captured by the Russians on the other side of the Causeway Heights. All he could see were the guns at the far end of the valley. He pointed out to Nolan "the uselessness of such an attack and the danger attending it."

Captain Nolan, who also couldn't stand Lord Lucan, apparently replied, "Lord Raglan's orders are that the cavalry should attack immediately."

Of course, the whole order, both written and spoken, was misinterpreted. Raglan meant the Light Brigade to recapture the guns and redoubts on the Causeway Heights, not make the pointless charge down the valley with

> *Cannon to right of them,*
> *Cannon to left of them,*
> *Cannon in front of them*
> *Volley'd and thunder'd . . .*

as the poet Tennyson had it.

Somewhat befuddled, Lord Lucan passed his misinterpretation of the order on to Lord Cardigan, who saluted and trotted off murmuring something about the last of the Brudenell's (his family name).

The Light Brigade formed up, Lord Cardigan out in front, and most gallantly prepared for the charge. They began trotting down the field. The guns were silent. Cardigan never even glanced over his shoulder. Suddenly, seemingly out of nowhere, Captain Nolan came galloping out and, yelling and waving his sword, inexcusably crossed in front of Lord Cardigan—who was utterly enraged by the insubordination. Cardigan believed that Nolan was trying to take over leadership of the charge. In fact, Nolan probably had realized the mistake and tried to redirect the charge at the last minute. At that moment, the Russian guns opened up, and Nolan's words were lost in the ensuing thunder. Nolan died with the first volley.

Now Lord Cardigan rode on in a blind fury. Almost unhorsed by the last salvo of the guns before he reached them, Cardigan steadied himself and made it through the line of cannons. Lord Lucan did not send the heavy brigade in support, considering the charge ill-conceived suicide. After encountering some Cossacks, whom he did not consider worthy opponents for a general officer, Lord Cardigan broke back through the lines and trotted back down the valley, leaving his men to make the most of their misfortune. That night he enjoyed a champagne dinner on his private yacht, utterly convinced of his innocence in the ghastly affair. Of some 670 men who participated in the charge, there were 278 human casualties, and 335 horses were killed in the action.

**WHAT IT MEANT**

The Charge of the Light Brigade has inspired generations. It was one of the noblest follies in the history of warfare. It was the last action in the Battle of Balaclava, which also included the action known as the "Thin Red Line" and a successful but far less famous Charge of the Heavy Brigade.

**SALES LESSON**

Well, what can we possibly learn from such stouthearted lunacy? There are actually any number of truths to be gleaned from the affair—not least being the importance of good human relations, the nature of leadership, and the importance of teamwork and cooperation. I shall not take the lesson from the behavior of Lord Cardigan, who never looked back and then, having accomplished the objective, turned around and left the field to his subordinates. I shall concentrate rather on the nature and importance of internal alignment—within a selling organization—which requires all of the above: skillful human relations, strong leadership, and exceptional teamwork. Lord Cardigan is the exemplar of what not to do.

The chief lesson has to do mostly with the implementation stage of a sale: Unless there is corporate backing and internal alignment, an implementation *will* fail. One must not race ahead, blowing through resources, without the full support of the entire organization. The great thing in preparing for a major sale is that all the key players for the implementation are lined up behind the seller. Otherwise, you may win the deal but lose the relationship with the buyer owing to a failed implementation. It is vital that you put in more effort, not less, immediately after the sale.

A seller needs to align with the organizational leadership, project management team, and support structure in order to ensure a smooth implementation. It takes tact, excellent relational skills, and the ability to work in a team environment to make it work. If you have angered the research and development (R&D) folks, steamrollered your project managers, upset your leaders by spending freely in the quest for the sale, then you cannot rely on their support at the crucial moment. If you are not present to see it through, if you go off celebrating too early (which is not to suggest that Lord Cardigan considered the charge anything but an utter disaster), and neglect the account, all will not go as hoped. *Cuiusvis hominis est errare.*

# 16

## THE BUYING CYCLE: RESOLUTION OF CONCERNS
## (THE PARTING SHOT)

*You wound, like Parthians, while you fly,*
*And kill with a retreating eye.*
—SAMUEL BUTLER, "AN HEROICAL EPISTLE OF HUDIBRAS TO HIS LADY" (1678)

The Battle of Carrhae, fought in Persia in 53 BC between the Parthian Empire and the Roman Republic, was one of the most crushing defeats in Roman history. The cunning Parthian cavalry rode up to the Roman legions, clashed, then turned and fled in apparent defeat. Galloping away from the Romans, who broke ranks to pursue, the Parthians shot arrows over their shoulders and decimated the Romans. The Roman Crassus, of the First Triumvirate, was killed when truce negotiations turned violent. The *Parthian shot* has come down to the modern age as "a sharp, telling remark, act, gesture, etc. made in departing."

The sales lesson is that you must not count your chickens before they hatch. The competition may look like they're on the run, but they may have something clever up their sleeve. The Parthian shot can have powerful consequences.

**WHAT HAPPENED** Marcus Licinius Crassus was the wealthiest man in Rome at the time he joined the First Triumvirate with Caesar and Pompey. He also may have been the worst general officer in Roman history. But that did not stop him from yearning to be covered in military glory (there is a lesson here about self-awareness and knowing what you are good at, but that is for another day). His ill-conceived campaign against the Thracian gladiator Spartacus in the Third Servile War had been generally regarded as a disaster, even though he eventually put down the revolt by sheer persistence and a nasty—and seldom used—policy of decimation as punishment for Roman defeats. In decimation, every tenth legionary was dispatched by his fellow legionaries. A bad general and a sore loser. Lovely.

Thus, when the "sure thing" opportunity arose to conquer the Parthian Empire, Crassus couldn't resist. He refused an offer by Armenian King Artavasdes II to invade Persia through Armenia and chose instead to march his army through the Mesopotamian deserts. "Here Crassus seemed to commit his first error, and except, indeed, the whole expedition, his greatest; for, whereas he ought to have gone forward and seized Babylon and Seleucia, cities that were ever at enmity with the

Parthians, he gave the enemy time to provide against him" (Plutarch, *Lives of Illustrious Men*, "Crassus"). When at last Crassus met the Parthian cavalry in pitched battle at Carrhae, he managed (read: caused) one of the most terrible defeats in Roman history and lost his life for his pains, which likely spared his surviving troops another round of his sore losing punishments.

The Parthian Surena, Crassus' adversary, was "in wealth, family, and reputation, the second man in the kingdom, and in courage and prowess the first . . . [and] he had a great name for wisdom and sagacity, and, indeed, by these qualities chiefly, he overthrew Crassus, who first through his overweening confidence, and afterwards because he was cowed by his calamities, fell a ready victim to his subtlety" (Plutarch, *Lives of Illustrious Men*, "Crassus").

The Battle at Carrhae came as a bit of a surprise to Crassus, who had for some days forced his infantry to keep up with his cavalry, when they accidentally came upon the entire Parthian Army. "First, as Cassius advised, he opened their ranks and files that they might take up as much space as could be, to prevent their being surrounded, and distributed the horse upon the wings, but afterwards changing his mind, he drew up his army in a square, and made a front every way, each of which consisted of twelve cohorts, to every one of which he allotted a troop of horse, that no part might be destitute of the assistance that the horse might give, and that they might be ready to assist everywhere, as need should require" (Plutarch, *Lives of Illustrious Men*, "Crassus"). Thus they marched toward Surena's main army. On crossing a small river, Crassus was urged to give the men rest, but he refused. As they approached the Parthian army, they were pleased to discover what appeared to be a not so impressive display of arms, for the Parthians had hidden their armor with coats and skins. Suddenly the Parthian drums began to roar like wild beasts and crash like thunder.

"When they had sufficiently terrified the Romans with their noise, they threw off the covering of their armor, and shone like lightning in their breastplates and helmets of polished Margianian steel, and with their horses covered with brass and steel trappings" (Plutarch, *Lives of Illustrious Men*, "Crassus"). The Parthians attacked the first line of Romans with lances, but the Romans held their ground. So the Parthians feigned retreat in disorder and quickly surrounded the Roman square before the Romans had figured out what was going on. "Crassus commanded his light-armed soldiers to charge, but they had not gone far before they were received with such a shower of arrows that they were glad to retire amongst the heavy-armed, with whom this was the first occasion of disorder and terror, when they perceived the strength and force of their darts, which pierced their arms, and passed through every kind of covering, hard and soft alike" (Plutarch, *Lives of Illustrious Men*, "Crassus").

The Parthians literally ran circles around the Romans, shooting armor-piercing arrows and causing much destruction. Every time the Romans broke ranks to attack them, they "threw their darts as they fled, an art in which none but the Scythians excel them, and it is, indeed, a cunning practice, for while they thus fight to make their escape, they avoid the dishonor of a flight" (Plutarch, *Lives of Illustrious Men*, "Crassus").

At last the Parthians employed a maneuver for which history remembers them: the Parthian shot (now often used in the corrupted form: the *parting shot*). The Parthian cavalry attacked and then feigned full retreat in the face of the Roman cavalry. The Romans pursued them in disorder. "The horse thus pushing on, the infantry stayed little behind, being exalted with hopes and joy, for they supposed they had already conquered, and now were only pursuing; till when they were gone too far, they perceived the deceit, for they that seemed to fly, now turned again, and a great many fresh [arrows] came on" (Plutarch, *Lives of Illustrious Men*, "Crassus"). In other words, the retreating horsemen turned their torsos 180 degrees on their horses and shot backwards while galloping away. It is said that in all, 20,000 Romans perished, and 10,000 were taken prisoners. Crassus was among those killed. He lay as an example "of inconsiderateness and ambition; who, not content to be superior to so many millions of men, being inferior to two, esteemed himself as the lowest of all" (Plutarch, *Lives of Illustrious Men*, "Crassus"). His death led ultimately to the civil war between Caesar and Pompey.

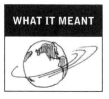

The Parthian cavalry has given its name to the Parthian (or parting) shot:

**Parthian shot**: a sharp, telling remark, act, gesture, etc. made in departing.

The death of Marcus Licinius Crassus marked the final blow to the Roman Republic. It resulted in a cooling of relations between the remaining two members of the First Triumvirate, Gaius Julius Caesar and Gnaeus Pompeius Magnus, or Pompey. The clever Pompey married into the house of a staunch political opponent of Caesar and was elected sole Consul in Rome in 52 BC, while Caesar was off fighting a revolt by Vercingetorix in Gaul. Caesar returned to Rome, crossing the Rubicon in 49 BC with his 13th Legion, classically saying *"Alea jacta est."* Civil war broke out and ended with the decisive Battle of Munda in Spain in 45 BC and Caesar's undisputed control of the Roman Empire. This ushered in the age of Imperial Rome.

There are a great many lessons that can be learned from bad leadership such as was displayed by old Crassus—the master of poor generalship. But we shall look here to the lesson of the Parthian shot: Don't count your chickens before they've hatched. One should not, as it were, break ranks at the tail end of the evaluation of options in the buyer's decision cycle on the assumption that the win is made. Now is the time that the buyer enters the *resolution of concerns* phase of the decision cycle.

There are two ways that the Parthian shot can take one by surprise in the complex sale: The first is by the competition, and the second is internal to the buying process within the company (account) itself.

In the first case, imagine a bake-off. The buyer has narrowed his or her choices for a vendor to maybe three. Our salesperson presents first and focuses the presentation on the unsurpassed quality of his or her product. This salesperson sits down smiling after enjoying nods of agreement from his audience. His or her product is in fact superior in quality, and the salesperson believes he or she has blown their socks off. This salesperson is quite certain that he or she has won the day. But the last presentation, by a formidable competitor, ends with the simple parting shot: We are never late. The audience responds. It is a crushing blow to our salesperson because the buyer relies heavily on just-in-time logistics. If the part is late, the assembly line shuts down. It is that critical to the operation. Our intrepid salesperson is stricken. He or she never said anything about being on time. And to make matters worse, his or her company is pretty good at just-in-time supply. Not great, mind you, but relatively decent.

Our seller has made a strategic error. He or she never fully understood the buying organization's decision criteria (which I shall discuss in some detail in Chapter 19). And as a consequence of the competitor's parting shot, the salesperson may just have undone all his or her good work over the last several months.

The second case is more difficult, but it can be mitigated. It is difficult because the parting shot is likely to occur behind closed doors. It is rarely, if ever, done in the salesperson's presence. It happens typically in the resolution of concerns phase of the buying cycle, when risk becomes the dominant concern in the buying organization.

Resolution of concerns begins when the buyer has chosen the frontrunner, the company with which he or she is most likely to do business. The salesperson from the chosen company is informed of the pending deal, and then fear—not to say panic—sets in on the buyer's end. Suddenly risk becomes the driving thought in the mind of the buyer:

"Have we chosen the right vendor?"

"Are we paying too much?"

"Will we disrupt the business unwarrantedly?"

"Who am I going to upset? Can I afford their displeasure politically? Am I risking my career?"

Understandable. The bigger the decision, the more risk there is associated with it. As the decision to sign the contract approaches, the level of angst rises. At Huthwaite, we call these large concerns—the penalties and risks the buyer believes could result from a decision in the seller's favor—*consequences*. Sometimes they are shared with the seller, but much more often they lurk beneath the surface, wreaking havoc on the buyer's thought process. They are a psychological strain. Unless these consequence issues are recognized, brought to the surface, and dealt with, the decision is in jeopardy.

The parting shot that undoes the sale may occur in a meeting of the buying committee. It even may be an offhand remark that the ultimate decision maker recognizes (or at least takes) as a warning. He or she suddenly is of the considered opinion that his or her career is on the line. He or she stops taking the salesperson's calls and begins to stew.

What, then, is the job of the salesperson? The salesperson's strategic objectives during the resolution of concerns phase of the buying cycle are threefold:

1. To discover whether consequence issues exist
2. To uncover and clarify any consequence issues
3. To help the customer resolve consequence issues

Now a word of clarification as pertains to the third item: The seller cannot in fact resolve the issues, but he or she can only help the customer resolve or become comfortable with them.

The first and most obvious signal that consequence issues might exist is a renewed concern with price. It is usually a smoke screen for deeper issues. When the buyer starts arguing price after the tentative decision has been made, it is time to probe for the underlying concerns. But there are other signs. The resurfacing of previously resolved issues is one. Unjustified postponements is another. Refusal to meet with the seller is a pretty sure sign, as is the sudden withholding of information.

So what is the best way for the seller to handle consequences? There are several basic principles. The first thing is not to ignore the possibility that consequences exist. Find out and deal with them. Do not just keep the old head low and hope that they go away on their own. They won't, and the deal could be lost. The second principle is to build trust and relationship early in the sales process. It is terribly important that the buyer feels a certain confidence that honesty with the seller will in fact be the best policy. The third thing is to remember not to try to resolve the issues for the buyer. He or she owns them, and he or she therefore must resolve them. The seller can only create the right conditions to allow the buyer to resolve his or her fears for himself or herself.

There are three deadly sins related to handling consequences. Here is how not to deal with them:

1.  Do *not* make light of the buyer's concern by denying its importance or by offering baseless reassurance.
2.  Do *not* prescribe a solution to the issue; it will only create resistance.
3.  Do *not* pressure the buyer for information or decisions.

If the salesperson can learn whether consequences exist, get them on the table (by being trustworthy and having a policy of full disclosure), and help the customer to resolve them (largely by avoiding the deadly sins), then he or she will be well on his or her way to defending successfully against the Parthian shot, whether it is internal or external. If you are wise and vigilant, you will make it through the resolution of concerns phase with colors flying. *Trahimur omnes laudis studio.*

# 17

## DEFENSE OF LITTLE ROUND TOP— BATTLE OF GETTYSBURG U.S. CIVIL WAR (1863)

### ON HANDLING THE MOTIVATION DIP

*Desire is the key to motivation, but it's determination and commitment to an unrelenting pursuit of your goal—a commitment to excellence—that will enable you to attain the success you seek.*

—MARIO ANDRETTI

The 20th Maine Volunteer Infantry Regiment, commanded by Colonel Joshua Lawrence Chamberlain, defended the far end of the Union left flank on the second day of the Battle of Gettysburg. They fought from the high ground of Little Round Top, which was repeatedly assaulted by Confederate forces. When running low on ammunition, they finally won the battle by staging a dramatic downhill bayonet charge. What's remarkable about the story is that Chamberlain, only weeks earlier, had to integrate the mutineers from the 2nd Maine Infantry Regiment into his unit. He was spectacularly successful.

The *motivation dip* is an inevitable feature of implementation. When it comes time for the true test of commitment to a new solution, motivation is the first thing to wane when the going gets tough. It is handled by preparing the customer for the moment when it comes.

**WHAT HAPPENED**

On the morning of the second day of fighting at Gettysburg—July 2, 1863—the Union left flank was exposed owing to some crossed signals and the confusion of troop shifting. Little Round Top, the hill at the end of the line (which held the key to the developing battle), was left completely undefended. When Colonel Strong Vincent was apprised of the situation, he immediately moved his brigade up the hill. Colonel Joshua Chamberlain's 20th Maine Regiment took up position at the extreme left flank. It has been said that had 10 more minutes elapsed, the Confederate Army would have commanded the hill on the far left flank of the Union Army. The outcome of the battle and indeed the war might have been very different.

The 20th Maine Regiment was comprised of 386 soldiers, 120 of which were seasoned veterans from the 2nd Maine Infantry Regiment—which had been disbanded recently, causing a mutiny by the men who had mistakenly signed on for three years, whereas the majority had signed on for only two years and were going home with the flag. The 120 mutineers were sent to Colonel Chamberlain with orders to shoot them if they refused to march. Instead, he gave a rousing and heartfelt speech on freedom and what it means to be an American.

"Some of us volunteered to fight for [the] Union. Some came in mainly because we were bored at home and this looked like it might be fun. Some came because we were ashamed not to. Many of us came . . . because it was the right thing to do. All of us have seen men die. Most of us never saw a black man back at home. We think on that, too. But freedom . . . is not just a word. We're an army going out to set other men free" (excerpt from Michael Shaara's, *The Killer Angels*).

The speech had its effect.

The fight for Little Round Top was intense that day. It culminated when Chamberlain's men were just about out of ammunition, and the line was almost broken by two Alabama regiments. Color Sergeant Andrew Tozier, who was later awarded the Medal of Honor for his bravery, kept the flag flying and held the line long enough for Chamberlain to order a bayonet charge down the hill. Tozier had been one of the mutineers from the 2nd Maine, whom Chamberlain had elevated to the dangerous but coveted post of flag bearer. The bayonet charge swung like a hinge—creating a simultaneous frontal assault and flanking maneuver. It was a massive success and turned the tide of the battle. Colonel Chamberlain also received the Medal of Honor for his valor that day.

**WHAT IT MEANT**

The successful defense of Little Round Top was the turning point of the Battle of Gettysburg, which was the turning point of the Civil War. The initiative was now—and for the rest of the war—with the Union Army.

**SALES LESSON**

The lesson here has to do with preempting the inevitable *motivation dip*. When a customer buys a new product or service, he or she goes through certain stages during implementation of that new product or service. First is the "new toy" phase, during which the customer "plays" with the gleaming "new toy." It is a time of excitement and experimentation, a time in which a common refrain is, "Let's see what this baby can do!" But it wears off and is followed by a much less interesting, much more difficult *learning stage*, which—if handled properly—is followed by the finally rewarding *effectiveness stage*. The trouble is that one stage does not follow inevitably on the other, for the learning stage can be fatal to an implementation. This is so because of the motivation dip, which is in fact inevitable in the learning stage.

Consider any new endeavor: Learning to play the violin, learning a new swing in golf, taking up a new hobby, or even going on a diet. Any of these is initially very exciting. The novice has great fun playing with the new task at hand; it is all new and shiny and thrilling. But when the hard work of actually learning sets in, motivation wanes. It becomes difficult, a chore. The amateur hobbyist loses interest, the golfer trying to correct a slice starts pulling his or her shots to the left, the fledgling violinist hears only moans and angry screeches from his or her best efforts with the horsehair. This is the motivation dip. It is a natural part of human psychology. But it must be handled, or all is lost. It takes a brazen hardheadedness and courage to overcome. But it can be done. Research shows that the best way to handle the motivation dip is to prepare the neophyte beforehand: Let the learner know that it will come without fail and encourage him or her to bull his or her way through.

There are three generally successful methods for handling the motivation dip, all of which were used to excellent effect by Colonel Chamberlain at Little Round Top. The first is to start before the contract is signed. Chamberlain prepared his men for glory by successfully integrating the 2nd Maine mutineers into his regiment some weeks before the defense of Little Round Top.

The second strategy is to involve the customer. Do as Colonel Chamberlain did by elevating young Tozier to Color Sergeant—mount a preemptive and peremptory defense against the motivation dip. Leave no room for weakness or doubt. When passion fades and courage falters, when ammunition dwindles, customer involvement is the best defense.

The third strategy is to put in effort early and often. Do not leave it to others to experience the motivation dip alone. Lead the charge. *Audaces fortuna iuvat.*

# 18

## ON VULNERABILITY ANALYSIS

*The essence of combat is to strike at the vulnerabilities of one's opponent. There is no "fair" or "unfair."*
—SAITO HAJIME (FROM SAMURAI X)

The Battle of Crécy (or "Cressy" in English) was a resounding triumph of superior Anglo-Welsh weaponry and tactics over vastly superior French numbers. Edward III led a small force of approximately 12,000 men against several times as many Frenchmen. It was longbows against mounted, heavily armored knights—and against conventional wisdom, the knights lost. Badly. Longbow archers were relatively new to the continental battlefield.

The sales lesson is that it is often possible to penetrate armor that is widely considered impenetrable. The great thing is to recognize vulnerability using *vulnerability analysis* and then ameliorate it.

The Hundred Years War had its roots in the conquest of England in 1066. William the Conqueror, Duke of Normandy, won the English Crown at Hastings. As king, he conquered and eventually controlled all England; as duke, he controlled a large part of northern France—but was a vassal of and owed fealty to the French King Philip I. The situation lent itself to complicated loyalties and no end of bickering that carried on through the years.

By 1308, things had not gotten much better. Edward II, the weak and ineffectual king of England, married Isabella of France. This made him Duke of Aquitaine, and thereby he technically controlled a large part of western France. It also made him a vassal of King Charles IV of France. When called on to do homage, Edward II made his son Edward of Windsor (later King Edward III of England) Earl of Aquitaine so that he could do obeisance in his stead. Edward II had a very precarious hold on England at the time and was afraid that if he went to France, he would lose his kingdom. He lost it anyway when his wife deposed him with the help of her lover, Roger Mortimer, in 1327. Best laid plans and all that.

Edward III was crowned King of England but ruled under the guidance of his mother and Roger Mortimer until he wrested control for himself. As grandson of King Philip IV of France (who was Isabella's father), Edward III reckoned he had a legitimate claim to the French throne. Philip VI, who had the support of the French barons and was crowned King of France on the death of Charles IV, disagreed and said so—and so the stage was set for the inevitable conflict.

Edward III eventually arrived in France in 1346 with little inclination to do homage and an army to reclaim the lands lost by his father. He was in no mood to be trifled with. His army marched north toward Paris, pillaging the place as they went. King Philip (or Philippe) VI, as you can imagine, was not amused and took the field with an army nearly three times the size of the English invasion force. The English skirted Paris and crossed the Somme River under heavy fire from a contingent of mercenary Genoese crossbowmen. They continued marching north, hotly pursued by the French army.

The English army was exhausted by now and running out of food. Sickness was spreading among the troops. Edward decided to turn and fight. He chose high ground near the market town of Crécy-en-Ponthieu. The front was about 2,000 yards long, stretching from the Maye River—which protected Edward's right flank—across terraced fields in the center to the village of Wadicourt on the left. It was a longish front for the size of the army but ideally suited for defense. Edward rested the army, and his men even managed to cook and eat before the French army appeared on the horizon.

The French army was quintessentially feudal. It consisted of several thousand knights who owed allegiance to the king because they held land at his pleasure. They amounted to heavy cavalry because they were heavily armed and arrayed in shining armor; they were both brave and experienced. Many fought under their own banners and therefore were impatient of any central command or discipline. With them, however, were many thousand poorly armed and poorly trained peasants who were conscripted by these knights, their masters. Also with the army were the aforementioned contingent of Genoese crossbowman and several foreign allies—most notably King John of Bohemia. On the whole, it was an undisciplined army of individual glory hunters.

The English army was very different, almost "modern" in the sense that the soldiers were professionals—paid to serve. Armed similarly to the French peasantry, except for the Welsh longbow archers, they were both trained and disciplined. And while in many cases sick and bootless, they were nevertheless rested and fed.

The same cannot be said of the French army, which proceeded from forced march to battle with nary a break between. King Philip had tried to halt them but, owing to miscommunication or pure disobedience, had been unsuccessful.

The Genoese crossbowmen were the first to see action. They surged ahead of the main French army and went on the attack. Unfortunately for them, their bolts fell short of the English lines. The arrows from the longbows that were shot in return fire, by contrast, found their mark. They took a dreadful toll on the crossbowmen, who realizing that they were outperformed turned and fled for the supposed safety of the French lines. The French knights did not see eye to eye with the crossbowmen on the matter of discretion being the better part of valor and proceeded to cut them down for cowardice. The carnage that ensued was made worse by the merciless stream of arrows from the Welsh longbows, which "fell like snow" on their targets.

The French were nonplussed but eventually managed to assemble for the first of many cavalry charges that were repelled successfully by the armor-piercing arrows from the longbows.

The right side of the English line was commanded, at least nominally, by the teen-aged son of Edward III, who was, owing to the peculiar dearth of English royal names, also called Edward. Known to history as the "Black Prince," young Edward was looked after by his tutor, Godfrey Harcourt, whereas his division in actual fact was commanded by the earls of Warwick and Oxford. The Black Prince acquitted himself well that day and is said to have won his spurs at Crécy.

The center, further back on the hillock, was commanded by the king himself. From his position, he could see the whole field as the battle unfolded and was able to reinforce the left or the right with equal ease. The left was commanded by the veteran warrior the Earl of Northampton.

Wave after wave of French knights were cut down in all their splendor by the unforgiving arrows from the longbows, deadly at

200 yards. As night fell, the English slept under arms, unaware of the extent of the destruction they had rained down on the flower of French nobility. When the fog cleared the next morning, all was revealed. The French were utterly devastated. The noble King John of Bohemia had fallen with untold thousands of French knights and peasant soldiers. The English had lost but a few hundred killed and wounded.

**WHAT IT MEANT**

Crécy was easily the worst defeat in French history up to that time. It marked a change in medieval warfare as longbows broke the rules of classic chivalry. Knights no longer died face-to-face at the hands of their peers but could be killed at a distance, anonymously, by yeoman archers.

The Black Prince, out of reverence for brave King John, took the Bohemian crest—three ostrich feathers—as his own. It is the crest of the Prince of Wales to this day. Crécy marked the end of an era and the beginning of nationalism. The English began to see themselves as Englishmen, distinct from Frenchmen, and vice versa.

**SALES LESSON**

As it turned out, French knights were vulnerable to Welsh arrows. Vulnerability in sales happens when a seller is considered to be weak (by the buyer) in a particular area that is important to the buyer, whereas the competition is seen as strong (by the buyer) in that same area. It makes for an at least uncomfortable position for the seller and often ends the sale completely.

A vital input to a salesperson's competitive strategy for any account is a structured understanding of how he or she stacks up against competing suppliers; what are the real strengths and weaknesses? This is where *vulnerability analysis* comes in. There is a simple and effective tool that points out vulnerabilities, as illustrated in Figure 18.1. There are three scales. The left-hand scale represents the buyer's decision criteria, ranging from crucial at the top to incidental at the bottom. The center scale is the seller's product or service in terms of the criteria, *as the seller believes the buyer sees it*, on a scale of strong at the top to weak at the bottom. The right-hand scale is the main competitor's product or

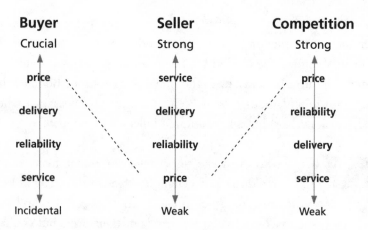

**FIGURE 18.1 Vulnerability Analysis**

service in terms of the criteria, again *rated from the buyer's perspective*, on a scale of strong at the top to weak at the bottom. Whenever a V shape emerges, as with the "price" criterion in the illustration, the seller is vulnerable. The deeper the V, the greater is the danger.

Let's say that our seller is selling a state-of-the-art printer/copier. Economy is very important to the buyer, and our seller's product is expensive, whereas the main competitor is relatively cheap. Our seller appears to be in a pretty weak position: He or she is vulnerable. Vulnerability analysis is an easy way to assess competitive vulnerability. Not only does it pinpoint vulnerabilities, but it also can help the seller to consider the strategic options that he or she can use to compensate for a vulnerability or overcome it. In this case, it becomes fairly obvious that the strategic goal is to increase the importance of "service" in the mind of the buyer. Later chapters shall consider strategies for handling vulnerability.

Buyer concerns are part of every major sale. Understanding where weaknesses lie enables sellers to predict where the competition will attack them and therefore what objections will arise. This, in turn, allows them to prepare arguments and/or alternative solutions to address those objections. Better still, the seller may be able to prehandle the objections and weaken the attack. There are three classic objections in major sales.

**Buyer**      **Seller**

Crucial      Strong

Incidental      Weak

**FIGURE 18.2** The Performance Gap

## 1. THE PERFORMANCE GAP

There is a performance gap when the buyer thinks that $X$ is crucial but believes (correctly) that the seller is not good at it. In this case, the seller must strengthen the performance of his or her product or service or else minimize the importance of $X$.

The seller can use

- Overtaking
- Redefining
- Strengthening Performance

Strengthening performance is done back at the shop, where the selling organization actually does a better job at producing the product or service. This is, of course, the most difficult approach—but it will pay the most dividends in the long run.

## 2. THE CREDIBILITY GAP

There is a credibility gap when the buyer thinks that $X$ is crucial but believes (incorrectly) that the seller is not good at it. I shall consider this in some detail in Chapter 20. The seller must correct any misperceptions.

**FIGURE 18.3** The Credibility Gap

The seller can use

- Referrals
- Site visits
- Documented reports
- Testimonials

## 3. THE RELEVANCE (OR VALUE) GAP

There is a relevance gap when the buyer agrees that the seller is good at $X$ but sees it as unimportant. The seller must help the buyer to see the

**FIGURE 18.4** The Relevance (or Value) Gap

value of $X$. The seller can try to develop the buyer's need into a problem worthy of action by using implication questions or need-payoff questions and benefits.

An understanding of these gaps, or objections, is critical to a right understanding of one's competitive vulnerability—and a right understanding of one's competitive vulnerability is vital to good strategic planning. Without knowing where he or she stands in relation to the buyer and to competitors, a seller is at an enormous disadvantage. The great thing is to face up to vulnerabilities, take them by the horns, and wrestle them into submission.

Had the French knights at Crécy understood their own vulnerability to the longbow, they may have been able to mitigate somehow and avoid the disaster that befell them. Because they viewed themselves as invincible, they charged to their own destruction. Had the English accepted the conventional wisdom that knights were invulnerable, they may never have ventured much in the pursuit of their aims. The great thing is to face up to honest strength or weakness, threat or opportunity, and do what is necessary to skew it favorably to the cause. The great thing is to understand that competitors always will be better at some things. The trick is to learn how to control the environment. *Caveat aemuli.*

# 19

## BATTLE OF THE ICE
## ALEXANDER NEVSKY VERSUS
## THE TEUTONIC KNIGHTS (1242)

### COUNTERING VULNERABILITY:
### INFLUENCING DECISION CRITERIA

*An inner process stands in need of outward criteria.*
—LUDWIG WITTGENSTEIN

The Battle of the Ice, between the Republic of Novgorod and the Livonian branch of the Teutonic Knights (mostly Estonians), was fought largely on the surface of frozen Lake Peipus. Nevsky chose the battlefield based on his knowledge of the surrounding terrain and his ability to hide cavalry and reinforcements on the shore of the lake.

In sales, choosing the field of battle is like understanding and influencing the decision criteria so that you take on the competition where you are best suited to compete.

**WHAT HAPPENED**

Early in the thirteenth century, Pope Innocent III declared a Baltic Crusade against the pagans of the north and the Russian Orthodox Church, which he feared was gaining inroads in northern Europe. Although the northern crusades were largely about land acquisition from the standpoint of the Teutonic Knights, who took the lead in the enterprise, there was some solace from the fact that the Pope had kindly extended the promise of eternal life to participants. The Baltic Crusades had faltered somewhat until they gained new life when Bishop Hermann von Buxhoeveden of Dorpat (Tartu) took Pskov in 1240. Meanwhile, Prince Alexander Nevsky of Novgorod was fighting (and defeating) the Swedish Army on the banks of the Neva River to the East. Nevsky returned from the East and retook Pskov in 1241.

In the spring of 1242, the lakes of northern Russia were still frozen. Apparently so were the hearts of the Livonian Teutonic Knights and their fellow Crusaders who had finally consolidated enough power to threaten Novgorod's holdings near the present Russian border with Estonia. Prince Nevsky met the Crusaders at the narrow strait that joins Lake Peipus with Lake Pskovskoe. On the morning of April 5, Alexander Nevsky feigned retreat in order to lure the Crusaders to a fight in the place of his own choosing—on the frozen lake. The knights, though they were slightly outnumbered, charged Alexander's carefully laid out position in a giant wedge formation. The battle that ensued has gone down in Russian history as ледовое побоище, the "Battle of the Ice."

Nevsky formed his lines on the eastern shore of the frozen lake at Raven's Rock. The Crusaders charged his position with between 2,000 and 4,000 knights, who were met on the ice by the Novgorodian infantry. They fought hand to hand for hours until everyone was exhausted from fighting on the slippery ice. Then Alexander brought out fresh archers from hiding and decimated the Crusader wings, which forced the Crusaders to begin to give way and soon to retreat in disarray. Then the appearance of fresh Russian cavalry from the shore turned the retreat into a general rout.

**WHAT IT MEANT** While contemporary accounts make no mention of the ice breaking under the heavily armored Crusaders, Sergei Eisenstein's epic movie, *Alexander Nevsky,* has the ice cracking and the knights crashing through into the dark depths. Regardless of whether many Crusaders were drowned, there is no dispute that the utter defeat ended Teutonic aspirations in Russia for many centuries. Indeed, it is neither ironic nor accidental that Eisenstein's immortalization of the battle came out in 1938, when Moscow was worried about a German invasion. Grand Prince Alexander Nevsky was sainted by the Russian Orthodox Church in 1547. *In magnis voluisse sat est.*

**SALES LESSON** The great lesson for us is *choose where to engage.* Or in the parlance of sales, influence the decision criteria to put yourself in the best possible position for defeating the competition. Stated more formally, there are three strategic objectives to keep in mind during the evaluation of options phase of the buying cycle (the overall objective, of course, is to emerge as the leading competitor). One should aim to

1. Uncover the factors or decision criteria customers intend to use to make choices between alternative ways to meet their needs.
2. Ascertain the customer's perception of how you and your competitors stack up against their criteria.
3. Influence the customer's decision criteria to maximize the perceived fit between their criteria and the strengths of your capabilities.

This is the most competitive phase of the decision process. A salesperson would be well served to understand the factors that customers will use to judge between alternative approaches to meeting their needs. Once the salesperson has a good idea of the competitive landscape, he or she can take action to influence it in his or her favor.

In order to understand these strategic objectives, it is important to understand the psychology of decision making or how people make choices. When choosing between alternatives, people generally go through three clear stages:

1. Identifying differentiators
2. Establishing the relative importance of differentiators
3. Judging alternatives using differentiators

The first step is not always as simple as it may appear at first blush. Suppose that an office manager is asked to replace the current printer/copier with a "newer and better" one for the office. Having dealt for a long time with the old one, he or she is pretty sure that a good service contract is high on the list of what matters. And service needs to be fast and reliable. The office does a great deal of printing, and down time is a luxury the office cannot afford. But what of the features of the printer? Is the quality of the printer in terms of high resolution more important than the speed it churns out pages? The state of the art in printing has literally dozens of features that may or may not meet the particular needs of the office in question. The office manager will need to analyze the needs of the business and choose the right criteria to use in the decision.

There are two important elements that make an effective differentiator or decision criterion. Obviously, the first one is that the customer can use the criterion to differentiate between the options. That is to say, some options will be inferior to others on the particular point. If all the options appear to be the same, it is not a good criterion. Unfortunately, in the modern age, so many products and services look exactly the same to the customer—and therefore price becomes the only differentiator.

The second element that makes an effective decision criterion is that it relates in some way to the customer's needs. It's no good having the fastest two-sided printing if the customer only prints on one side of the page. But then, if the customer is green conscious and only prints on both sides of the page, this would be an excellent differentiator.

Having identified the right decision criteria—which both meet the needs of the office and can be used to differentiate between alternative options—the buyer is ready to rank the differentiators in order of importance to the business. Some features, such as the quality of the printer and its reliability, are already known to be crucial and therefore move straight to the top of the list. Speed and versatility may fall next in order. While photo-quality color printing may matter occasionally, it is more of an incidental and so falls lower on the list. Price may fall somewhere in the middle because the boss has his or her heart set on the newest, fanciest machine available—but certainly doesn't want to break the bank.

Once the customer has worked out the list and decided on his or her criteria in order of importance, the judgment process begins. The customer begins to compare each of the competing alternatives against his or her list of decision criteria. He or she compares the relative strengths and weaknesses of each product against the ranked list. The product that most closely matches the list—strengths more or less matching up with crucial criteria and weaknesses more or less matching up with more incidental items—is most likely to win. The buyer may never do any of this on paper, but it is very much on his or her mind.

Such is the decision criteria and how they are arrived at. But what has this to do with the seller? It's simple. If the seller understands the psychological steps that the buyer is going through, he or she can influence the buyer along the way. The buyer may need to back up in his or her judgment process if, for example, none of the alternatives can meet what he or she believed to be the most critical factor. Such a buyer may have to back up and reassess the importance of his or her criteria. He or she simply may have to accept the fact that with greater speed comes less reliability. This is where the seller comes in, asking questions that help the buyer to really understand what's actually possible. No alternative option can be best at everything. The seller ought to help guide the buyer through the alternatives. Then he or she can influence the decision criteria in favor of his or her own product. This is why I don't recommend responding blindly to requests for proposals (RFPs). The selling organization that is in on crafting the RFP is already likely the chosen option, and the request is for form's sake.

The seller can begin influencing decision criteria even early in the recognition of needs phase of the buying cycle. During this phase of the cycle, the seller's strategic objective is to uncover and develop customer needs in areas where his or her products or services can provide the best solution. In doing this, the seller also begins the process of influencing the customer's decision criteria. Let's say that the seller's copier is the fastest on the market. It's likely that during the recognition of needs phase, this seller will ask problem and implication questions to uncover customer dissatisfaction with the speed of the existing equipment. If the seller's questions succeed, the customer will feel a distinct need for the fastest alternative. Thus, when the customer begins thinking about differentiators, speed will be topmost in his or her mind. Because speed is a legitimate customer need, and it happens to be where the seller shines, it will make an excellent decision criterion when the time comes.

One last important fact about decision criteria: They live on after the sale. Unlike needs, which are met by the purchase of the needed product or service, the decision criteria continue to be important to customers long after the sale is made. Usually, in fact, they live on into the next cycle. This is possibly why successful salespeople give considerable attention to decision criteria when they sell. The durability of decision criteria makes them especially important in the development of long-term business in major accounts. Influencing a customer to use a decision criterion that favors his or her product or service will give a salesperson a continuing competitive advantage.

So there it is. For the reasons stated, influencing decision criteria is the strategic objective during the evaluation of options phase of the buying cycle. Its importance in the complex sale cannot be overstated.

Like Prince Alexander, a salesperson must do everything in his or her power to control the environment in which he or she competes. There are four basic strategies for influencing decision criteria by reducing the importance of the crucial ones. The first rule is to accept that the criterion is legitimately important.

1. *Overtaking* recognizes that it is dangerous to challenge a crucial criterion and concentrates instead on building up the importance of other criteria.
2. *Redefining* allows the crucial criterion to remain important to the customer but alters its definition so that the seller can meet it more easily.
3. *Trading off* accepts the importance of a criterion but shows that there are other factors that must be balanced against it.
4. *Creating alternative solutions* recognizes that the criterion is important and therefore searches out new and creative ways to meet it.

Prince Alexander Nevsky understood the importance of strategic advantage and so chose the shoreline by Raven's Rock as the most defensible position on frozen Lake Peipus. He knew the terrain and chose very wisely. He won magnificently based largely on controlling the environment in which he competed.

# 20

### COUNTERING VULNERABILITY:
### INCREASING STRENGTHS

*Strength does not come from physical capacity. It comes from an indomitable will.*
—MAHATMA GANDHI

After John Huss and Jerome of Prague were burned at the stake for heresy by the Council of Constance, John of Trocsnow asked King Wenceslas if he could avenge this tyranny by Pope and Emperor. So began the Hussite Wars, the patriotic struggle for Bohemian independence from the Roman clergy. During those wars, Zizka became one of the great heroes of history. His troops were passionately attached to him and fought ferociously for the joint causes of reformation and independence. Their valor and willingness to be martyred in the cause made them all but invincible.

The sales lesson is about increasing the customer's perception of the seller's strength. One of the ways to do this is by correcting any misunderstandings. Sometimes the customer rates a seller as weak because of a misunderstanding or because the customer's information about his or her products or services is inaccurate. The seller must help the buyer see the truth. Of course, sometimes the customer sees the seller as weak in a particular area because the seller's company is weak. There the seller must increase strength.

**WHAT HAPPENED**

In 1415, the great Bohemian church reformer John Huss was burned at the stake by the Council of Constance. His death stirred deep antipapal feelings in the Czech people—in none more than in John of Trocsnow, chamberlain to Queen Sophia, the wife of King Wenceslas IV in Prague.

John of Trocsnow is better known to history as John Zizka ("one-eyed" in the Bohemian dialect of the time) because he had lost his left eye early in life, probably in a brawl. As the son of lower nobility, he spent his early youth at the court of King Wenceslas. Later he served as a mercenary in armies all over Europe, but mostly in the Danish and Polish armies, which paid handsomely. He fought beside the Poles at Tannenberg in 1410 when they crushed the Teutonic Knights. He returned to the court at Prague in 1412, and he became a fervent follower of Huss at that time. As such, he was profoundly disturbed by the treatment of Huss by the Council of Constance (which, incidentally, on the plus side of the ledger at last solved the Western Schism—there were three popes at the time).

By 1419, Zizka had taken some leadership in the Hussite indepen-dence movement in Bohemia and is said to have led the attack on the Prague councilors, who were thrown from the third story window of the New Town Hall into a crowd of Hussite protesters. This was the First Defenestration of Prague. The shock of the event apparently sent King Wenceslas into an apoplectic fit, and he died of a stroke. He was suc-ceeded as King of Bohemia by his brother Sigismund, who happened also to be Emperor of the Holy Roman Empire (and King of Hungary, etc., etc.). Sigismund had presided over what was now widely regarded in Bohemia as the foul murder of John Huss. Soon thereafter began the bloody and ferocious Hussite Wars.

Zizka gathered an army of peasant farmers and left Prague, marching for Plzen, where he hoped to find a suitable fortress as headquarters for his new military community. He had become de facto general officer of the Taborite faction of the Hussite rebellion. Plzen turned out to be a bad situation, so Zizka concluded a truce with the royalists that was supposed to allow him safe travels to a new stronghold at Tabor. He left the city with 400 peasants-turned-soldiers, a dozen wagons, a few horsemen, and many women and children. The women acted as nurses and cooks and in quite a few cases fought alongside the men. It was quite a spectacle.

As it happened, a contingent of royalist lords, accompanied by some 2,000 knights in full armor, rode out to intercept and destroy Zizka's small army. They apparently did not consider themselves bound by the terms of the truce and figured that they could quite easily nip this rebel-lion in the bud. Indeed, they did not even expect to fight, being of the considered opinion that they could simply ride the farmers down and trample them underfoot of their warhorses. They were in for a surprise.

Zizka, as it turned out, was something of a military genius. In fact, he is one of the few commanders in history who never lost a battle. And it seems that he had given a great deal of thought to the question of how to defeat heavy cavalry ever since Tannenberg. His thinking was about to pay off.

The "Iron Knights" of the Roman (royalist) party arrived in and took control of Pisek, where Zizka had hoped to stop off for supplies and hopefully even some reinforcements. Soon it became evident that he was going to have to fight—against vastly superior numbers of seasoned warriors. A lesser man might have crumbled. Zizka merely surveyed the landscape and chose an almost perfect defensive position near the village of Sudomer. He drew up and chained together the wagons at the top of a fairly steep incline, flanked on one side by a small dam that had been built to create shallow fish ponds that spread out to his right. He had armored the wagons so that they created a sort of mobile fortification that horses neither could leap over nor smash through. The wagons were manned with field artillery (which had been used before during siege operations but had never before been employed by infantry on the medieval battlefield), pistolas (wildly inaccurate handguns that nevertheless were effective against a massed cavalry charge), and crossbows. Most of the Hussite soldiers wielded traditional farming instruments that had been modified for warfare: grain flails with metal tips, pitchforks, hoes, and hammers. Zizka reckoned that these tools, in the hands of people who already knew how to use them, could be just as deadly as pikes and poleaxes. In addition, of course, as they understood it, they had God on their side and therefore fought with tremendous zeal and no fear of death.

The first wave of Sigismund partisan knights attacked the iron-clad wagons head on but had to dismount to get up the hill, where they were met with fierce resistance. Any who managed to get close enough were clobbered by flails. The pistolas used by the Hussites, by the way, were so cumbersome that a knight actually could see the bullet approaching. The bullet moved that slowly—just a little faster than a rock from a sling (which the children used to great effect). The knights retreated in vexation and probably shame.

The second charge came through the ponds, but the horses got bogged down in the mud, and again the knights had to dismount. They, too, in their heavy armor got a bit stuck in the mud. They were easy targets for the Hussites who had been positioned on the dam and closed on the knights with extraordinary vim and vigor. At last night fell, ending the battle. It had been particularly bloody with a lot of Hussite casualties for such a small force, but many more royalists were killed in the action. The Hussites kept the field, signifying victory.

The Battle of Sudomer was the first real engagement of the Hussite Wars and the first victory for Zizka as commanding general. While it was a small engagement, it served as the foundation for the Zizka legend. His reputation was made, and it grew massively with each successive victory. Some believed that Zizka was a warrior angel of God; some even said that by a miracle the sun set early on Sudomer. Others were convinced that Zizka was a demon in human flesh, a feeling that grew when Zizka lost his good eye to an arrow at the siege of Rubi in 1421 and proceeded to lead his troops into battle completely blind. His army sang "Ye Warriors of God" while marching into battle, which became so famous that by the fifth crusade the king's army scattered when they heard the song—before they even saw the Hussites.

**WHAT IT MEANT**

As fate would have it, Zizka contracted the bubonic plague while besieging Pribyslav and died in 1424. His legend lived on. Eventually, the Hussites split into factions and were finally destroyed in 1434.

Zizka had begun what became known as the infantry revolution. He introduced field artillery and invented the tank. He was also the first to "circle the wagons"—a maneuver put to great use by settlers of the American West and that came to be known as the strategic *laager* in the Boer Wars of South Africa.

As followers of Wycliffe and Huss, the Hussites laid the groundwork for the Reformation.

**SALES LESSON**

At Sudomer, Zizka did what might be called *increasing strength*. The enemy had an incorrect perception of his strength. He proceeded to school them.

*Increasing strength* is the second of three strategies used for countering vulnerability:

*Strategy 1:* Change the decision criteria (see Chapter 19) so that areas in which you are strong become more important to the customer.

*Strategy 2:* Increase strength (which I shall discuss presently).

*Strategy 3:* Diminish the competition (which I shall discuss in Chapter 21).

FIGURE 20.1  **Strategies for Countering Vulnerability**

Increasing strength becomes necessary when a seller can't meet a buyer's crucial decision criteria or when a buyer has a misperception of the seller's strength. As mentioned in Chapter 18, I call this a *performance gap* when the buyer has a critical decision criterion and believes correctly that the seller can't meet it. That is to say, the seller cannot in fact meet it. I call it a *credibility gap* when the buyer believes some decision criterion to be absolutely vital but is incorrectly under the impression that the seller is not good at it.

I have found that there are at least four ways to increase strength:

1. *Improve your product or service* (when there is a performance gap). That is to say, get better at what you provide and/or how you provide it. If the buyer sees the seller as weak in a particular area— and the seller is in fact weak in that area—then the first option for the seller's company is to improve in that area. There is no trick to it.

2. *Create alternative solutions* (when there is a performance gap). If a buyer accurately believes that the seller's organization cannot meet a crucial decision criterion, the seller needs to be imaginative and creative. While it is not necessarily easy, when it works, it is one of the most effective ways to handle difficult decision criteria issues. It involves probing for the real need underlying a decision criterion and then seeking to meet that need with a surprising and sometimes unconventional alternative approach. The crucial decision criterion in Figure 20.1 is quality. Suppose that the buyer is shopping for a printer. The seller's product has a well-deserved reputation for breaking down regularly. In probing on the question of quality, the seller discovers that the real reason quality is an issue is because downtime costs the printing company a bundle in lost production. The seller might suggest that his or her company could provide an on-site technician to keep the machine up and running. This alternative solution might meet the case.

3. *Negotiate* (when there is a performance gap). Another way to potentially increase strength is through negotiation. If, as in Figure 20.1, the issue is quality, it may behoove the seller to offer an excellent service contract that will mitigate the problem with quality. The offer reduces the perceived weakness. Negotiation plays a legitimate and often helpful function in varying the terms of an offer so that perceived strength is increased.

4. *Correct any misunderstandings* (when there is a credibility gap). It does happen that a buyer rates a seller as weak in an area in which he or she is in fact strong. These misperceptions can come from misunderstandings or sometimes inaccurate information. Unfortunately, the seller can't correct a misunderstanding merely by assertion. In order to correct a misunderstanding or misperception, the seller must offer *proof* that his or her product is not in fact weak in the particular area. To do this, the seller can use

- *Referrals/testimonials.* Previously satisfied customers offer a great rebuttal to bad information.

- *Site visits.* Clear, first-hand information is a terrific way to correct a buyer's perceptions.
- *Documented reports.* Third-party industry articles or reports also can provide solid evidence in favor of the seller's product or service.

The imperial army in the Battle of Sudomer labored under a misapprehension of Zizka's strength. The army was in a difficult position because Zizka's army was in fact weak in areas that the imperial army had perceived it to be weak (i.e., size, training, experience, etc.). But Zizka was a master at creating alternative solutions (e.g., using zealotry to maximum effect and adapting tactics, weaponry, and armaments to the battlefield) and thereby increasing strength to achieve victory. *Audere est facere.*

# 21

## COUNTERING VULNERABILITY:
## DIMINISHING THE COMPETITION

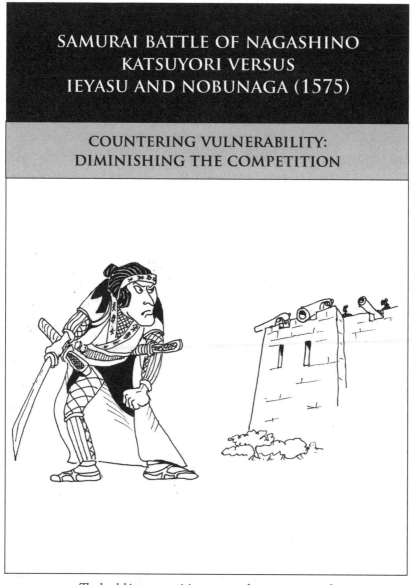

*The healthiest competition occurs when average people*
*win by putting in above average effort.*
— COLIN POWELL

The Battle of Nagashino pitted the famed Samurai cavalry charge against more or less modern firearms. Takeda Katsuyori had laid siege to Nagashino Castle in central Japan. A relief force consisting of the armies of Tokugawa Ieyasu and Oda Nobunaga arrived and engaged Katsuyori on the plain of Shitaragahara. A rainstorm the night before the battle, which left the ground muddy and a small river across the plain, convinced the relief force that it could withstand a cavalry charge. The relief force built a palisade 50 yards from the river to protect a matchlock corps of 3,000 gunners. The charge got bogged down in the mud and at the creek, and the advancing force was finally destroyed by large-scale volley fire (the first recorded use of such a tactic worldwide) in three ranks, which allowed the defenders to rain continuous matchlock fire into the cavalry ranks from behind the palisade. Katsuyori was defeated.

The sales lesson is about diminishing the competition to counter your vulnerability. The most difficult—and certainly the most dangerous—strategy for reducing vulnerability is to attack the perceived strength of your competitor so that the customer no longer feels that the competitor is strong. This needs to be done generically and indirectly so as not to destroy your own credibility.

**WHAT HAPPENED**

Sixteenth-century Japan was the time of *Sengoku-Jidai,* the "age of the country at war." The emperor in Kyoto had been purely a ceremonial figurehead for several hundred years, and the Ashikaga Shogunate had lost any real power beyond Kyoto after the Onin War late in the fifteenth century. Japan was a feudal society ruled by warlords (or *daimyos*—"great names") exercising power over small, autonomous states throughout the provinces.

By 1575, several of the most powerful *daimyos* included such Samurai warlord luminaries as Oda Nobunaga, Tokugawa Ieyasu, and Takeda Katsuyori—who was brave and reckless and had almost limitless ambition for the Takeda clan. On June 16, 1575, Katsuyori began a prolonged assault on Nagashino Castle, which was held for the Tokugawa by 500 men under the leadership of young Okudaira Sadamasa. The castle sat on the high ground at the confluence of the Onogawa and Takigawa rivers, which protected the southeast and southwest sides. The northeast and northwest sides were protected by walls and moats. Katsuyori stormed the ramparts to the north but was repelled by the brave defenders. He then tried to mine the walls but was thwarted by a successful countermining effort. He tried sending Samurai across the rivers on rafts, but that expedition came to naught. He tried siege towers, but they were destroyed by the valiant Tokugawa partisans. Finally, he launched a general assault that also failed. He was nonplussed but decided in the end to starve out the defenders. He crisscrossed the rivers with ropes and built walls to block escape from the north.

On June 22, Sadamasa sent out a volunteer to try to reach Tokugawa Ieyasu with news of the siege and a plea for relief. The volunteer escaped by the river, slicing the ropes with his dagger. He reached Ieyasu and reported the now rather grave situation at Nagashino Castle. Ieyasu rallied his ally Nobunaga to the cause, and they promised to set out for Nagashino with a relief expedition the following morning.

The intrepid volunteer headed back to bring the good news to the castle but was captured trying to cut the ropes in the river again. He nevertheless managed by subterfuge to get the message of relief to the castle.

Nobunaga arrived with an army of 30,000—10,000 of whom were trained arquebusiers (matchlock men). Ieyasu brought 8,000 men. Their opponent, Katsuyori, led an army of only 15,000. Nevertheless, he determined to stay and venture all on his Samurai cavalry in a pitched battle. The Takeda clan moved into battle formation at 5:00 a.m. on June 29, 1575. It was to be a momentous day. Their leaders, fearing the worst, had drunk a farewell toast with their comrades the night prior.

Nobunaga had prepared his defense about a mile away in the foothills of Mount Gambo. He built palisades just on the far side of a small stream to protect his arquebusiers from the invincible Takeda cavalry charge. His plan was to keep them hidden behind the palisades rather than be more honorably visible. He handpicked 3,000 of his best matchlock men and divided them into three 1,000-man divisions. They held their fire (quite literally because matchlock rifle fuses were lit by a burning match) until the last possible moment. When the time came, they opened fire in volleys of a thousand. The first rank fired and could almost be reloaded before the third rank even fired. The result was a truly devastating continuous fire into the ranks of the oncoming Samurai warriors at point-blank range.

The cavalry charge got a bit stalled in the rain-soaked ground and then again trying to cross the shallow Taki River just in front of the Oda breastworks. And then the cavalry was met with the nonstop fusillade from the matchlocks. The battle raged for 10 hours. By 3:00 p.m., it was all over. Nobunaga's defense had been a brilliant success. The Takeda Samurai had suffered a complete and humiliating defeat.

**WHAT IT MEANT**

The Battle of Nagashino in 1575 marked the beginning of the end of the Sengoku-Jidai. It laid the groundwork for the unification of Japan. In 1603, Tokugawa Ieyasu became Shogun. The Tokugawa Shogunate ruled a peaceful (with the exception of the Shimabara Rebellion; see Chapter 26) and completely isolated Japan for more than two centuries. The battle also marked the effective end of medieval warfare in Japan. The use of peasant soldiers armed with matchlocks and firing in volleys had rendered the invincible Samurai cavalry for the first time all but ineffective. Nobunaga's matchlock men were lowly peasants. Such a force could never have been expected to stand up against mounted Samurai. Of course, the Samurai Code—which barred anyone not a Samurai from carrying weapons—was instituted soon thereafter. *Aliam vitam, alio mores.*

**SALES LESSON**

The sales lesson from Nagashino is the third strategy for countering vulnerability: *diminishing the competition*. This one is a little bit tricky. A salesperson needs to tread lightly when talking about the competition. But it can and sometimes should be done. Nobunaga instituted a policy of diminishing the competition. The feared Samurai cavalry charge was widely held to be unstoppable. Nobunaga changed that perception by dealing with the issue head on. Salespeople may need to be a touch more circumspect, but the outcome is the same.

The main danger of talking to customers about the competition isn't just the potential loss of credibility; it is also the loss of crucial selling time. If you are talking about the competition, how can you be fully focused on understanding customer needs and decision criteria? If you end up getting sidetracked into discussing a competitor's product, you risk three things:

1. *Lowering your own image.* Especially if you are ahead of the competition in the customer's mind, you can only hurt your position by discussing your competitors.
2. *Opening up areas you can't control.* Discussion of a competitor's weaknesses also may open up a discussion of his or her strengths. This can only put you on the defensive, which is dangerous ground.
3. *Building the competitor's importance.* The more you talk about the competition, the more important the competition becomes in the mind of the customer. By keeping your competitors at the top of the customer's mind, you build them up, from which they can only benefit.

These risks suggest that the wise salesperson would be very careful about adopting a policy of attacking a competitor's strengths in order to reduce his or her own vulnerability. However, this is not to say that it should never be done—only that when it is done, it is done rather carefully.

There are two ways to weaken the competition successfully without doing damage to your own image. The first is to discuss competitive weakness indirectly. The second is to discuss generic weakness instead of naming a particular competitor. Both can do wonders at reducing the customer's perception of a competitor's strength without doing yourself damage.

There are times when you are pressured to talk about competitors' weaknesses because the customer asks a direct question about them. There are a couple ways to handle this. If the customer asks a direct question such as, "How does your product compare with the one offered by XYZ Corporation?" you essentially have two choices. You can respond with something along the lines of "XYZ Corporation's product is more expensive, slower, and has a poor service record." That is to say, you focus on the competitor's weakness. The other alternative is to get the customer thinking about your product instead of the competitor's by answering thus: "Our product is cheaper, faster, and has a superior service record." This answer conveys exactly the same information but has a much more benign psychological effect on the customer.

The first alternative may be seen as knocking the competition, which can hurt your credibility and can engender a feeling of defensiveness on the part of the customer. Moreover, it sets the customer on a path of thinking about the competitor and his or her product rather than your own. The customer may respond by mentioning some of the strengths of the competitor—opening a discussion that may go badly for the unwary salesperson.

The second alternative is preferable because it indirectly attacks the competitor's weaknesses by focusing the customer on your own contrasting strengths. Of course, it only works if you actually have contrasting strengths. If your product is not actually superior to the competitor's, the strategy falls down. One of the problems with a commoditized world is that all products tend to look the same to the customer—even when there are legitimate differences.

There is another, in some ways better, strategy for lowering the customer's opinion of the competition's product, and that is to expose generic weaknesses. Don't talk specifically about XYZ Corporation and its product but rather discuss the generic weaknesses of the processes, methods, materials, or whatever else that XYZ Corporation uses in its products or services. By using this strategy, you can attack the general weaknesses from which your competitors suffer without directly criticizing them. You can say quite a bit that may be really quite negative without penalty and still come across as objective and professional by describing the flaws inherent in certain ways that things are done in your industry. Again, this only works if your own company uses a genuinely better approach.

While some very successful salespeople are able to diminish the competition effectively without damage to their own reputation, these two strategies—discussing competitive weaknesses indirectly and discussing only generic weaknesses—ought to be used most cautiously. As a general rule, it is much more expedient and often more effective when seeking to counter vulnerability to either influence decision criteria or build up the customer's perception of your own strength.

# 22

## BATTLE OF KIRCHOLM
## WINGED HUSSARS VERSUS
## THE SWEDISH ARMY (1605)

### ON MAXIMIZING DIFFERENTIATORS

*All sciences are now under the obligation to prepare the ground for
the future task of the philosopher, which is to solve the problem of value,
to determine the true hierarchy of values.*
—FRIEDRICH NIETZSCHE

In the autumn of 1605, King Charles IX of Sweden laid siege to the port city of Riga in Latvia. Lithuanian Hetman, Charles Chodkiewicz—one of the all-time great cavalry commanders—assembled an army a few miles south of the city near a town called Kircholm. Charles IX brought a numerically superior force down to meet him. After several hours of skirmishing, Chodkiewicz feigned retreat to lure the Swedish army off the high ground. It worked. The Commonwealth (Polish-Lithuanian) cavalry, the Winged Hussars, formed up and charged the advancing Swedish army. The charge was devastating in the extreme and frankly scared the hell out of the Swedes, who folded like a tent. *Alta alatis patent.*

The sales lesson is on maximizing differentiators. The Commonwealth cavalrymen wore wings into battle, appearing to their foes not unlike an army of angels. Genuine differentiation can make an enormous difference, especially in a commoditized world. Your sales force itself can be the differentiator by the way your salespeople sell.

**WHAT HAPPENED**

In 1599, Sigismund III Vasa was deposed from the Swedish throne by his uncle, Charles IX of Sweden. This broke the Polish-Swedish union that had existed under Sigismund since 1592. Though still King of the Polish-Lithuanian Commonwealth, Sigismund wanted Sweden back. His ambitions set off the Polish-Swedish War of 1600–1611.

Charles IX arrived in Latvia in 1605 and laid siege to Riga with a large Swedish army, including a number of Scottish, Dutch, and German mercenaries. Lithuanian Hetman John Carol Chodkiewicz brought an army of just about 3,500 to relieve the city. The Polish-Lithuanian Commonwealth forces set up camp near the village of Kircholm on September 26, 1605.

The Swedes attempted to surprise the enemy in the night, but the Polish-Lithuanian Commonwealth camp was alerted by the watch. So, instead, the Swedish army (approximately 11,000 strong with 11 cannons) waited for sunrise on September 27 to form up on the heights above Kircholm. The Swedes were numerically superior (about 3:1) and were in an advantageous defensive position. Charles was in no hurry to move.

Hetman Chodkiewicz tried to provoke the Swedes from the heights by sending up skirmishers and light artillery, but to no avail. Finally, Chodkiewicz feigned a retreat. This was more successful. The Swedish king ordered the attack. As the Swedes raced uphill, they were staggered by the heavy fire of the Polish-Lithuanian Commonwealth infantry muskets and cannon.

Then Chodkiewicz ordered a charge of the Polish-Lithuanian Commonwealth heavy cavalry—the splendid Winged Hussars. It was decisive. It was a complete rout. The battle was decided in 20 minutes. The Polish-Lithuanian forces were victorious. This is remembered in Poland as the greatest triumph of Polish cavalry ever.

King Charles IX was himself wounded but escaped. All the artillery and 60 banners were captured. Polish-Lithuanian Commonwealth losses were minimal compared with the Swedes.

**WHAT IT MEANT**

It was an astonishing victory for the Polish-Lithuanian Commonwealth. King James I of England, the Turkish sultan, and even the Pope sent congratulations to Chodkiewicz.

The siege of Riga was lifted, and the Swedish army withdrew.

The unpaid Polish-Lithuanian army revolted, so Chodkiewicz was unable to press the advantage. The war dragged on, and Sigismund never did recover the throne of Sweden.

The reputation of the Winged Hussars was firmly established for all time. It is said that they were undefeated in battle for over a century.

**SALES LESSON**

The Winged Hussars provide the lesson: It is on *differentiation*. They were unlike any other cavalry of their time— they were differentiated by the wings they wore. In sales, the definition of differentiation has changed dramatically. It used to refer to the way that salespeople convince their customers that their products and services are different— and superior—from the competition in ways that matter most to the customers. This no longer works.

Not so long ago a seller was expected to be an expert on his or her own products and services. It was enough to know the product or service the seller sold inside and out and to know how it could benefit customers. Such knowledge and expertise satisfied most buyers, who relied on sellers chiefly to provide product and service information. This is no longer true. Buyers have raised the bar; they are more demanding.

Today, the seller who is *only* an expert on products and services is summarily dismissed as a talking brochure and, as such, an anachronism. This is so because buyers now can find any information that may interest them about products online. They no longer need to see sellers to learn about the latest bells and whistles. Today, the seller needs to bring substantially more to the bargaining table.

First of all, to most customers, it looks like everyone is offering the same thing. When they look across the landscape of what's being sold, they don't see differences. Salespeople may see differences because they know the competition and they know themselves, and they know that there are differences. But the world all looks black and white to customers. And therefore, they just want the cheapest option.

An enormous number of new products fail to meet the projections that Wall Street expects or the projections that stakeholders care about. More and more new products fall flat because they take too long to get off the ground. And by the time they do, competitors are already there. Products and services are simply unable to sustain differentiation in most cases. Competitors arrive with the "me-too" versions ever faster. More and more buyers care only about price. Companies are trying desperately to develop corporate strategies that will keep them somewhere in the zone of uniqueness. There are still differences in products and differences in services—for a short while at least. But the market doesn't credit it anymore.

The forces of commoditization have picked up speed. Customers have much more information than they ever had before. The huge amount of information available about products and services and the ease of access to it have created a general impression of commoditization, even where it doesn't really or needn't exist. Sifting through and sorting out the torrent of information, everything begins to appear homogenized. Customers don't have time to sort through the subtle differences. So they get to the point where everything looks the same. And it actually is true that everything does begin to look the same.

Try a little experiment. The results might surprise you. Go to your company's website and to those of your top five competitors. Copy the "About Us" or "Who We Are" sections of the six websites, and paste them into a document. Scrub them of brands and logos. Then see how many people in your organization can identify the copy from your own website. You may find that there's not much to differentiate any of the products or services or even the sites that offer them.

Let's take a look at the old versus the new definitions of differentiation. It used to be possible to differentiate offerings based on the product or the service itself. The product itself embodied value, which meant that selling was really about communication. It wasn't about creating value. Whoever had the best talk track and the greatest slide deck, whoever did the fanciest demonstration, could win the day—provided that his or her product was in any way different from that of the competitor.

But today customers have disengaged from the idea that the product creates the value. What they expect now is to get something from that selling organization that's not in the product or service. Now the differentiator is the seller himself or herself. If the seller doesn't do something to embody a greater sense of value in the customer, then the customer doesn't need him or her. And the customer will default to buying on price.

In the old definition of the complex sale, the customer had a lot of different decision makers involved, there was a relatively long purchasing cycle, and the decision had risk. There was a risk associated with making the wrong choice. The risk was having too little information. Now the risk is different. The complex sale still involves multiple decision makers, it still involves a long sales cycle, but the risk perceived by the customer today is the risk of having too little *insight*. The risk is in not having a good enough understanding of the world in which they are competing. And therein lies the clue to how salespeople can sustain differentiation: It is by the *way* they sell, not *what* they sell. It has become ever more critical for sellers and sales organizations to differentiate themselves by *the way they sell*.

Today, the seller has to be able to provide insight. It is insight that sustains differentiation. The exchange of goods and services for money happens almost by the way. Customers are trading on the salesperson's expertise. The value-creation strategies outlined in the section on the four value drivers (Chapters 5–8) are illustrations of how that insight or expertise plays out in the relationship between buyer and seller. Customers are ever so much more sophisticated. They will pay a premium for insight, analysis, and expertise that they cannot get anywhere else but from the sales experience.

# 23

### ON EFFECTIVE NEGOTIATING BEHAVIORS

*However, even during the preparations for action, we laid our plans
in such a manner that should there be progress through diplomatic
negotiation, we would be well prepared to cancel operations at the
latest moment that communication technology would have permitted.*
—HIDEKI TOJO

In 1791, the United States imposed an excise tax on whiskey as part of Treasury Secretary Alexander Hamilton's plan to centralize and fund the national debt. Pennsylvania farmers, who could only get their corn to market economically by distilling it into whiskey, revolted. The Whiskey Rebellion ensued, resulting in the tarring and feathering of more than one unhappy tax collector. The insurrection reached its pinnacle in 1794, when a heterogeneous army of dissidents led by one David Bradford marched on and occupied Pittsburgh. George Washington himself gathered and sent an army to quell the rebellion, which quickly dissipated before the army arrived. The central issue from the government's perspective was how to enforce on a local level national laws passed by Congress.

The lesson from the Whiskey Rebellion has to do with *effective negotiating behaviors*. Much of the unpleasantness might have been avoided if western congressmen had done a proper job of negotiating on behalf of their constituents rather than caving to federal (and some might argue elitist) interests.

**WHAT HAPPENED**

On March 3, 1791—not quite two years after the opening of the first U.S. Congress on April 1, 1789—the House passed the Whiskey Act by a vote of 35 to 21, following a rather heated debate. The act was an excise tax on whiskey and was supremely unpopular on the western frontier of the fledgling United States. Although enacted by their duly elected representatives, farmers in the western counties of Pennsylvania (not to mention Virginia, North Carolina, Kentucky, and Georgia) thought it an unacceptable burden and an unfair imposition— not unlike the hated Stamp Act of 1765, which had, in part, sparked the recent War of Independence. The Pennsylvania farmers rose up in a brief but momentous armed revolt.

The tax was the brainchild of Treasury Secretary Alexander Hamilton, who was looking for ways to reduce the now-federal debt that had been incurred by the several colonies during the late unpleasantness with the English Crown. It was actually quite a clever plan to concentrate tremendous wealth in the hands of a few affluent financiers, in the hope that they would help to put the United States on a solid economic footing. This would be done by collecting money from the populace at large and funneling it in the form of interest payments to these prosperous speculators in public debt.

The rebels objected on the grounds that this tax was what we would call a *regressive tax*—which because applied uniformly takes a larger percentage from low-income people than from high-income people. And it was aimed at producers rather than consumers. Ordinary farmers reckoned that it was flat unfair.

Immediately after the tax went into effect, the trans-Appalachians reacted with some vim. They held protests, petitioned the government, and refused to pay. Occasionally, they just attacked revenue agents— in at least one notable case, they tarred and feathered an unlucky tax collector. Things continued generally unsettled until 1794, when federal agents started arresting tax evaders. Then it got downright ugly. A small group of rebels attacked the home of John Neville, the inspector of revenue for western Pennsylvania. After an exchange of gunfire, the attackers left—but they returned the next day with a much larger force. Neville was by now defended by 10 soldiers from Fort Pitt. During the ensuing confrontation, the leader of the insurrectionists was shot and killed.

On August 1, 1794, a lawyer named David Bradford assembled a militia of some 7,000 so-called whiskey rebels to march on Pittsburgh. The plan to put the city to the torch was foiled when the citizenry of Pittsburgh met the disgruntled frontiersmen not with guns but rather with venison, ham, and whiskey.

When news of the aborted attack reached the federal government in Philadelphia, President George Washington had had quite enough. He decided on a dual policy of negotiation and a show of overwhelming force. First, he sent a peace commission consisting of three Pennsylvanian negotiators. Then he raised a federal army of almost 13,000 troops under the command of Revolutionary War hero General Henry "Light-Horse Harry" Lee, the governor of Virginia. The army (known as the "Watermelon Army"), which was accompanied by Secretary Hamilton and included such luminaries as General Daniel Morgan and young Meriwether Lewis (of later Lewis and Clark Expedition fame), marched into western Pennsylvania. The opposition evaporated before the overwhelming show of force.

In the end, 20 obscure insurrectionists were arrested and taken to trial in Philadelphia. Two were found guilty of treason, but both were pardoned by President Washington in a show of magnanimity.

**WHAT IT MEANT**

Some consider the Whiskey Rebellion to have posed the greatest threat to the young republic between the Revolutionary War and the Civil War. It was actually a huge constitutional crisis. That the western counties might attempt to secede from the United States was a very real possibility. Washington had effectively asserted the power of Congress and the Constitution.

The revolt also helped to create the two-party system in American politics by throwing light on the great issues that defined the politics of the day: freedom versus security, agrarian economy versus commercial economy, the wild western frontier versus the staid eastern establishment, and the wealthy elite versus the democratic many.

Interestingly, the federal expedition to put down the rebellion cost the government $1.5 million—about a third of the total revenue from the Whiskey Tax, which was repealed by the Republicans in 1803.

**SALES LESSON**

Because of the nature of the rebellion, which included several attempts at settlement by negotiation and which began with a vigorous negotiation in Congress, we shall look at some of the *behaviors of successful negotiators*. Skilled negotiators use certain types of behaviors frequently, whereas they tend to avoid others.

*Irritators.* Certain words and phrases that are commonly used during negotiation have negligible value in persuading the other party but do cause irritation. Probably the most frequent example of these is the term *generous offer* used by negotiators to describe their own proposals. Similarly, words such as *fair* and *reasonable* and other terms with a high positive value loading have no persuasive power when used as self-praise while serving to irritate the other party because of the implication that the other party is unfair, unreasonable, and so on. Most negotiators avoid the gratuitous use of direct insults or unfavorable value judgments. They know that there is little to gain from saying unfavorable things about the other party during face-to-face exchanges. However, the other side of the coin—saying gratuitously favorable things about themselves—seems harder for them to avoid. Skilled negotiators tend to avoid such *irritators*.

Any type of verbal behavior that antagonizes without a persuasive effect is unlikely to be productive. Most people fail to recognize the counterproductive effect of using positive value judgments about themselves and, in so doing, implying negative judgments about the other party.

*Counterproposals.* During negotiation, it frequently happens that one party puts forward a proposal, and the other party immediately responds with a counterproposal. Skilled negotiators infrequently make immediate counterproposals. The common strategy of meeting a proposal with a counterproposal is not particularly effective. The disadvantages of immediate counterproposals are

- Counterproposals introduce an additional option, sometimes a whole new issue, that complicates and clouds the clarity of the negotiation.
- Counterproposals are put forward at a point where the other party has least receptiveness, being concerned with its own proposal.
- Counterproposals are perceived as blocking or disagreeing by the other party, not as proposals.

*Defend/attack spirals.* Because negotiation frequently involves conflict, negotiators may become heated and use emotional or value-loaded behaviors. I call such behavior *defending/attacking*. Once initiated, this behavior tends to form a spiral of increasing intensity: One negotiator attacks, and the other defends, usually in a manner that the first negotiator perceives as an attack. In consequence, the first negotiator attacks more vigorously, and the spiral commences. Defending and attacking are often difficult to distinguish from each other. What one negotiator perceives as a legitimate defense, the other party might see as an unwarranted attack. This is the root cause of most defending/attacking spirals. Skilled negotiators, if they decide to attack, give no warning and attack hard.

*Behavior labeling.* Skilled negotiators tend to give an advance indication of the class of behavior they are about to use. Thus, for example, instead of just asking, "How many units are there?" they might say, "Can I ask you a question—how many units are there?" thereby giving a warning that a question is coming.

Instead of just making a proposal, they might say, "If I could make a suggestion . . ." and then follow this advance label with their proposal. In general, labeling of behavior gives the negotiator the following advantages:

- It draws the attention of the listeners to the behavior that follows. In this way, social pressure can be brought to force a response.
- It slows the negotiation down, giving time for the negotiators to gather their thoughts and for the other party to clear his or her mind from the previous statements.
- It introduces a formality that takes away a little of the cut and thrust and therefore keeps the negotiation on a rational level.
- It reduces ambiguity and leads to clearer communication.

Skilled negotiators do not label their disagreement. They are more likely to begin with the reasons and lead up to the disagreement. One of the functions of behavior labeling is to make a negotiator's intentions clear, which is why skilled negotiators avoid making it clear that they intend to disagree. They normally would prefer their reasons to be considered more neutrally so that acceptance involves minimal loss of face for the other party.

*Testing understanding and summarizing.* Testing understanding is a behavior that checks to establish whether a previous contribution or statement in the negotiation has been understood. Summarizing is a compact restatement of previous points in the discussion. Both behaviors sort out misunderstandings and reduce misconceptions. *Clara pacta, boni amici.*

Skilled negotiators are concerned with clarity and the prevention of misunderstanding.

- *Reflecting.* Skilled negotiators tend to use testing understanding as a form of reflecting behavior that turns the other party's words back in order to obtain further responses, for example, "So do I understand that you are saying that you don't see any merit in this proposal at all?"
- *Implementation concern.* Skilled negotiators tend to have a great concern with successful implementation. They test and summarize in order to check out any ambiguities at the negotiating stage rather than leave them as potential hazards for implementation.

*Asking questions.* Skilled negotiators ask a significant number of questions during negotiation. Questioning techniques are important to negotiating success for some of the following reasons:

- Questions provide data about the other party's thinking and position.
- Questions give control over the discussion.
- Questions are more acceptable alternatives to direct disagreement.
- Questions keep the other party active and reduce his or her thinking time.
- Questions can give negotiators a breathing space to allow them time to marshal their own thoughts.

*Feelings commentary.* Skilled negotiators are often thought of as people who play their cards very close to the chest and who keep their feelings to themselves. This is not actually true. Skilled negotiators are quite likely to give information about their internal events.

The effect of giving internal information is that negotiators appear to reveal what is going on in their minds. This revelation may or may not be genuine, but it gives the other party a feeling of security because such things as motives appear to be explicit and aboveboard. The most characteristic and noticeable form of giving internal information is a feelings commentary, where skilled negotiators talk about their feelings and the effect the other party has on them. For example, the average negotiator, doubting the truth of a point put forward by the other party, is likely to receive that point in uncomfortable silence. Skilled negotiators are more likely to comment on their own feelings, saying something like, "I'm uncertain how to react to what you've just said. If the information you've given me is true, then I would like to accept it, yet I feel some doubts inside me about its accuracy. So part of me feels rather suspicious. Can you help me resolve this?" The expression of feelings is linked directly to establishing trust in counseling situations. It also seems to be true for negotiating.

*Argument dilution.* Most people have a model of arguing that looks rather like a balance or a pair of scales. In fact, many of the terms we use about winning arguments reflect this balance model. We speak of "tipping the argument in our favor," or "the weight of the arguments," or how an issue "hangs in the balance."

This way of thinking predisposes us to believe that there is some special merit in quantity. If we can find five reasons for doing something, then that should be more persuasive than only being able to think of a single reason. We feel that the more we can put on our scale-pan, the more likely we are to tip the balance of an argument in our favor. It's not true.

Skilled negotiators use few reasons to back up each of their arguments. Although the balance-pan model may be very commonly believed, it is actually a disadvantage to advance a whole series of reasons to back an argument or case. In so doing, the negotiator exposes a flank and gives the other party a choice of which reason to dispute. It seems self-evident that if a negotiator gives five reasons to back a case and the third reason is weak, the other party will exploit this reason in his or her response. The more reasons advanced, the more a case is potentially diluted. The poorest reason is a lowest common denominator: A weak argument generally dilutes a strong argument.

So that is more or less how successful negotiators behave.

# PART 3
# SALES MANAGEMENT

# 24

## DAVID AND GOLIATH
## ISRAELITES VERSUS
## THE PHILISTINES (1024 BC)

### CRM SALES FORCE AUTOMATION:
### ON CHOOSING THE RIGHT TOOLS

*If the axe is not sharp, it doesn't matter how hard the wood is.*
—CHINESE PROVERB

The story of David and Goliath is the classic victory of the underdog (which has a whole slew of psychology lessons in its own right). David was a young shepherd boy who went up against a giant Philistine from Gath on behalf of the Israelite King Saul. Saul had supplied his own armor and sword, but David was uncomfortable in the ill-fitting and heavy weaponry. So he took a sling and five smooth stones and went up and slew Goliath with one well-placed shot to the forehead.

The great sales lesson from the confrontation between the illustrious future king David and the giant Goliath is on the *importance of fit*. One needs the right tools, the right technology, to accomplish the task. It is not necessarily the latest or the shiniest new technology—it is the one that *fits* right. It is the one that works for you.

**WHAT HAPPENED**

In the fighting season of 1024 BC, the Philistine and Israelite armies were drawn up for battle, encamped on opposite mountainsides of the Valley of Elah. Each morning the Philistine champion came out and taunted the Israelites, decrying their army and indeed their manhood (catch any sporting event across the globe, and you can see how little has changed!). Each morning he demanded that an Israelite champion take him on in mortal combat. The deal was a simple one: The army of the loser would become slaves of the winner's army. So you can see that the risk/reward equation was pretty lopsided. The Israelites didn't like their odds one bit because the Philistine champion was Goliath, the giant of Gath. He apparently stood a little over 10 feet tall (6 cubits and 1 span—if you use the standard cubit of 20 inches and span of 9 inches), somebody you would love to have on your basketball team but not as an opponent on the battle field. The Israelites were understandably fearful of this colossus and endured over 40 days of insults and scorn being constantly tossed their way by the Philistines.

One day, a young shepherd boy named David came out to the Israelite army to bring food for his brothers and to collect news from the front. He heard the taunts of Goliath and was suitably outraged. He approached the Israelite King Saul and offered to do something about it. Saul was naturally skeptical as he took a look at David and then likely cast his eye back to Goliath yelling and stomping around in the distance.

On the other hand, he liked the shepherd boy's pluck and courage, even if he thought his chances of success were slim at best. But David persisted, telling tales of having bested lions and bears in defense of his sheep, and Saul eventually came round to the view that he needed to do something to shut the giant up, and seeing as nobody else was in a hurry to do it, he might as well give David a chance.

> Saul clothed David with his armor; he put a bronze helmet on his head and clothed him with a coat of mail. David strapped Saul's sword over the armor, and he tried in vain to walk, for he was not used to them. Then David said to Saul, "I cannot walk with these; for I am not used to them." So David removed them.
>
> Then he took his staff in his hand, and chose five smooth stones from the wadi, and put them in his shepherd's bag, in the pouch; his sling was in his hand, and he drew near to the Philistine [1 Samuel 17:38–40 (NRSV)].

The rest, as they say, is history. Goliath predictably loudly mocked the young David (who was only 16 years old). Handsome perhaps, he admitted, but a warrior? David, not wasting time on exchanging insults, simply responded with a rock from his sling that smashed into the giant's forehead and toppled him face down. And so ended Goliath and all his insults.

**WHAT IT MEANT**

Since then, the legendary battle between David and Goliath has captured the imagination of underdogs in every discipline of human endeavor. Every school boy who has listened to the story has imagined himself in David's shoes, slaying giants. Indeed, it is a story with many lessons.

This also was the beginning of Israel's ascendancy over the Philistines. Although warfare between the two Levantine powers continued on and off for years, the Israelites wrested power that lasted through the reign of Solomon, David's son. David, of course, gained tremendous prestige and popularity among his own people and was later crowned King of Israel. He was a warrior king and a poet and the stuff of legend. He wrote many of the psalms that are extant in the Hebrew (and Christian) Bible. In the Middle Ages, he was inducted as one of the Nine Worthies, the chivalric heroes of old. Not bad for a shepherd making a food delivery!

**SALES LESSON**

But what can we possibly learn about sales? The lesson I shall draw has to do with David's choice of technology— his choice of tools. We are not Luddites, far from it. Huthwaite has been on the leading edge of using technology to support salespeople. David did not dismiss the latest armor technology because he was against armor as a strategic tool. He rejected it because it was not the right tool for the task at hand. Had he gone lumbering out in heavy, ill-fitting armor, it is likely Goliath would have easily slain him before he could lift the sling and get his first shot off.

David was given a suit of armor that belonged to the king. It was the very latest in defensive technology. The helmet was bronze and shiny and beautiful. The chain mail was heavy and impervious to the latest weaponry. But it didn't fit. David couldn't maneuver in it. He could barely walk. He was given a bronze sword—the latest offensive weapon. No doubt sharp and weighty, it turned out to be too weighty and unwieldy. Again, David tried in vain to walk with the sword strapped to the armor. It simply was not the right fit for the boy. It was an excellent fit for the king—and would have worked perfectly for anyone of the right physical stature.

David took off the armor and lay down the sword. Without them, he could move with speed and agility. Without them, he was not overburdened by the latest tools of the trade. Without them, he was able to choose his own tools—five smooth stones and a sling. Not necessarily the latest in technology. Indeed, ridiculed by the giant, David was regarded as childish and old-fashioned for his choice of technology (whether the giant changed his mind in the nanosecond before the pebble made contact with his head we will never know). The sling was a weapon that David had used many times, that he knew to be both effective and efficient. He was willing to use it because it was time-tested and proven to work in dire and extreme circumstances. He could rely on it. And it did not fail him.

The same holds true in sales. If you opt for a technology that has all the bells and whistles and fancy applications but does not make your salespeople more efficient and help them to close sales, they will not use it or certainly will resent being made to use it. They will see it as time-consuming—and wasted time at that. You must choose tools wisely. Tools can greatly enhance opportunity management, account management, and forecast analysis. In fact, customer relationship management (CRM) tools have become *de rigueur* in the world of sales today. The trick is to find the right fit for your sales force. If you have a sales methodology, it should be reinforced by your CRM tools. The nearer your tools reflect a day at the office, the more likely your salespeople are to adopt them, use them, and win with them.

Let's take the case of CRM systems. Most companies today are struggling to convert leads into meetings and ultimately sales. Roughly half of all firms find that they are unable to turn more than half their leads into meetings. Without being able to get their foot in the door, nearly half the individual salespeople are under quota and suffering from diminishing opportunities.

In today's sales environment, with turnover nearing 30 percent and often with major travel restrictions being imposed, it is critical that each sales representative be given the tools and support needed to win the dwindling number of deals available. With more pressure and limited resources, increased sales productivity is the goal for managers, but it is an elusive goal because one-third of prime selling time is wasted by poor enablement. Even with CRM systems, many salespeople are not being given the right tools for their job.

Most salespeople see their CRM systems as a management application that is designed for executives and number crunchers rather than a tool that can be used to increase sales and help to perform tasks more effectively.

CRM systems were designed to aid organizations by managing and tracking records in one place, providing sales forecasting, and supporting management's leadership efforts. These programs and systems were going to reinforce best practices, measure the performances of individual salespeople accurately, encourage better internal and external communications, and ultimately improve sales and revenue figures.

In reality, most CRM systems have fallen short of these promises because (1) they are not being used effectively, and (2) they lack the essential tools and resources that salespeople actually need.

Unfortunately, the software-as-a-service approach generally has not improved CRM system usefulness or increased sales effectiveness. Despite recent studies that show a yearly sales increase of $57,000 from each representative by shifting just 10 minutes a week to more active selling time, salespeople are still struggling to get true value from CRM systems and make their time more productive. Additionally, a recent study found that 75 percent of companies reported that their CRM forecasts weren't accurate enough to be trusted. Even if a company has a CRM system in place and it is being used, this does not necessarily translate into having a more productive sales team or realizing increased revenue.

When salespeople are asked to use CRM systems, they generally drop their shoulders, roll their eyes, and in their mind kiss their valuable selling time goodbye. For them, it's anything but automation. For a big part of that day, they perceive themselves turning into a data-entry clerk inputting their deals into a seemingly redundant system only to turn around and discuss those same deals later in the week with their managers.

Instead of helping to focus representatives on their individual leads and providing tools to help them win the deals, CRM systems all too often generate information that is consumed by management but does not then get turned into helpful guidance for salespeople. While this automates the recording process and presents management with consolidated information on what their salespeople are doing, it does not actually aid in selling best practices and is often not used effectively, resulting in wasted effort and dubious, subjective forecasts.

Along with general past numbers and trends, companies often consider peripheral information and personal feelings when calculating future performance. When first-line managers start the process, they gather their salespeople's data and adjust the expected future numbers based on their knowledge of and confidence in each person under them. Some salespeople are overly optimistic, some overly pessimistic. This additional layer of subjectivity is then propagated by each level of the hierarchy. By the time the chief financial officer (CFO) considers the forecasts with a view to communicating with Wall Street or the board, those numbers bear little resemblance to reality and are a summation of how the individuals of the organization felt on the day.

So what is the answer? It should be obvious by now. The *right* CRM implementation is critical, and it must be adapted to their sales process and must make it easier for the salespeople to sell. It should cut down the amount of time the sales rep has to spend reporting on deals, and it should enable managers to access information without having to go to the rep directly. It ultimately should be simple and designed from a salesperson's perspective. As with many things in life, simplicity is the key. There is no written law that I am aware of that dictates the need for complexity in every software application deployed. Software can be made to be simple, intuitive, and effective. Look at what the late Steve Jobs did at Apple. His whole quest was for simplicity and utility. Thus, when you go to deploy any technology, be it a CRM system or otherwise, in support of your salespeople, ask yourself, "Is this going to weigh down my salespeople like an ill-fitting suit of armor, or is it going to give them a simple tool that can help them to hit the target quickly, first time?" *Non omnes qui habent citharam sunt citharoedi.*

# 25

## THE FEEL-GOOD FUNNEL:
## ON USING TIME WISELY

*Action expresses priorities.*
—MAHATMA GANDHI

In 451, while Attila besieged Orleans, his Huns plundered the sub-urbs. The Romans, under Flavius Aetius, arrived and fell upon the overladen Huns, routing them. They pursued the retreating Huns closely, attacking and devastating their rearguard. Attila would have been content to leave the region, but Aetius was spoiling for a fight. Attila therefore chose the essentially flat and open Catalaunian Plains near Châlons to turn and fight. But it was by now late evening, so the armies encamped for the night. When the sun rose, the Huns stayed in their wagons—not emerging until after noon. Attila is said to have waited to give his men a chance to retreat in the dark if they were beaten. They were indeed beaten. They encamped for the night, and Aetius—for political reasons—allowed Attila and his humiliated army to slink away the next morning.

When salespeople are trying to close very important sales, they ought not to spend all their time plundering the nearby low-hanging fruit. Rather, they should make sure that their sales funnel is clean, pri-oritize the valuable accounts, and thereby not get blindsided by a loss of their most valuable prospects.

**WHAT HAPPENED**

In the spring of AD 451, Attila the Hun was having a mar-velously fruitful spring in northeastern Gaul, plundering and pillaging to his heart's content. He had crossed the Rhine with a horde of somewhere between 300,000 and 700,000 Huns and Ostrogoths (and I think you'll agree that numbers like that are worthy of the moniker *horde*) and other assorted Germanic barbarians to test the polit-ical will of Imperial Rome to defend the Empire. He sacked a number of cities, including Rheims, Strasbourg, Cologne, and Worms (famous now for its Diet in 1521—a meeting, not a medieval weight-loss pro-gram). And then, leaving Paris to the Parisians, he laid siege to the city of Orleans. By this time, the horde was rather drunk with power and booty. It was beginning to go a bit soft. And sieges seem to have rather bored the men—after all, a horde is for marauding not sitting around. The horde took its time plundering the surrounding neighborhood and was taken by surprise when "the terror of Barbarians" (as Gibbons called him), the noble General Flavius Aetius, arrived on the scene with a veritable horde of his own. Sometimes referred to as "the last of the Romans," Aetius had put together an extraordinary and powerful alliance of Burgundians, Visigoths, Alans (the weak link), and of course, his own Roman legions.

The Huns (and Ostrogoths and other heathens) were in fact so surprised that they fled, heavily laden with their treasures. Some sources suggest that Attila, unwilling to be trapped beneath the walls of Orleans, executed a strategic withdrawal. Whatever happened, the Hunnic rearguard was harassed and practically destroyed while Attila's army marched into the Catalaunian Plains in present-day Champagne and into the darkness of evening. Both armies encamped on the plains near Châlons, preparing to do battle the following day.

Attila made his plans, and in the morning he refused to budge from his position behind the wagon train. He seems to have determined that a full day of fighting would not favor his chances against the massive Roman coalition, so he did not deploy his troops until about noon. No doubt he was hopeful that if fortune didn't smile on him that day, he could retreat as previously into the dark, good night. (The poet Dylan Thomas would have been proud.)

As so often happens in battle, fortune is a fickle mistress and this time did not in fact smile on Attila and his horde. In an epic battle, the Romans overtook the left flank, the Visigoth King Theodoric took the right flank, and together they crashed into the Hunnic center—which was hounding the Alans in the Roman center. Attila and his army retreated behind his wagons and were defended by archers until nightfall. Thus ended the Hunnic invasion of Gaul. The Romans had triumphed.

**WHAT IT MEANT**

It was the last victory of Imperial Rome. The next year, the Huns invaded Italy and ravaged the countryside. Rome, as an empire, was finished. But the Battle of Châlons (also called the Battle of the Catalaunian Plains) was a tremendous victory. It is said that Western Greco-Roman Christian culture owes its existence to Aetius' success on the fields near Châlons.

**SALES LESSON**

Let us focus now on the events (looting) that led to the great battle. Had Attila controlled his troops and stopped their riotous living, he may never have been caught off guard at Orleans. The troops had allowed themselves to become complacent with spoils aplenty and a seemingly rich pipeline of opportunities for more. See where I am going? We can draw somewhat of a parallel to the modern business-to-business (B2B) sales manager who, if he or she does not continually review his or her pipeline critically and challenge what is in there, allows his or her troops to become complacent and careless with properly qualifying opportunities and worse still not recognizing changes in the landscape (such as another competitor entering the field or their customers buying habits evolving).

There is one sure way to get accurate sales forecasts and ensure good pipeline management, and that is to put rigor into the system. The right customer resources management (CRM) system will help to separate the wheat from the chaff—if the salesperson can be trusted to enter accurate data. From a human psychology standpoint, though, the way to get accuracy is to avoid the trap of what I call the *feel-good funnel.*

The feel-good funnel is a sales pipeline that is full to overflowing with opportunities at each stage, especially the early stages, which creates a false sense of security around meeting quarterly to yearly targets. Unfortunately, owing to its counterintuitive nature, many organizations have as yet not come to embrace the concept that less is indeed often more. It continues to unknowingly frustrate sales leaders, embarrass salespeople, and cost companies all over the world millions of dollars in lost revenues every year. In addition, the insidious sales costs created by the feel-good funnel in terms of wasted sales effort, unnecessary travel expenses, poor resource allocation, and misuse of sales management cannot even begin to be calculated.

There are two commonly accepted measures for assessing the health of a company's sales pipeline:

1. *The number of opportunities in the pipeline.* This is measured either by the total number of opportunities or the number of opportu-

nities at each stage or both. In my work with sales organizations, I frequently hear managers state with confidence that to reach their annual revenue target, they have to have a prescribed number of forecasted deals in stage one, two, three, and so on. When asked how those target numbers are arrived at, there is often disagreement and confusion.

2. *The dollar value of the deals in the pipeline.* "We have to have $X million in stage one, $X million in stage two, $X million in stage three . . ." is a comment that I also hear frequently. As with item 1 above, there is often disparity as to the source of these target amounts.

While these two metrics are the ones used most commonly by sales organizations to measure pipeline strength, there is an underlying and damaging assumption with their use, which is that "More is better." Sales leaders have been conditioned to believe that purely having more opportunities in the pipeline and having a large dollar amount at each stage is a positive thing. How many times have you heard someone say, "It's a numbers game after all"? The feel-good-funnel syndrome is a result of this misplaced thinking.

I use the term *feel good* because as a sales manager looks ahead to his or her revenue target, it feels good to know that he or she has a sufficient quantity of opportunities in the pipeline to allegedly reach that target. A regional vice president can feel comforted believing that he or she has surpassed the target amount of dollars in the forecast. A senior vice president of sales can feel optimistic seeing that his or her teams supposedly have enough opportunities in the late-stage pipeline to guarantee short-term revenue and enough deals in early stages to predict with confidence that they will exceed revenue goals later in the year. And in the lean times when deals are not closing, it can become almost a comfort blanket: *Things might be tough now, but in a few months it will be okay, just look at the strength of the pipeline.*

The feel-good funnel typically has a lot of opportunities at each stage but is particularly overloaded in the early stages. Any experienced sales manager will say that of course there will be attrition as deals progress through the stages. But attrition will not be a problem because there are a sufficient number of opportunities and dollars in each stage that will emerge in the form of closed business. There is little need for a manager to be concerned. His or her salespeople have obviously been busy generating new business.

This is a funnel that gets the *quantity* targets right.

Unfortunately, failure to address the *quality* of opportunities in the pipeline effectively is where it all frequently falls apart. Placing emphasis on the quantity of deals in the pipeline over the quality of those deals directly leads to all-too-familiar scenarios. That is, opportunities that

1. Have been forecast at a late stage that, on further review, realistically should be forecast at an earlier stage.
2. Have significant revenue associated with them that, on deeper scrutiny, realistically should be forecast for a much lesser amount.
3. Have been forecast to close at a certain date that, when examined through the lens of quality and not quantity, should be forecast to close at a later, more realistic date.
4. Have revenue that gets pushed back month after month.
5. Should never have been included in the pipeline in the first place.

All these "opportunities" are frequent contributors to missed targets and embarrassing late forecast downgrades.

Examining the quality of early-stage opportunities before they progress through the pipeline is an essential task if an organization is to avoid the trap of sinking time, money, and resources into deals that are never going to close. Herein, though, lies another trap that sales organizations fall into when attempting to qualify opportunities. The salespeople concentrate on the activities that they can control in the sales process rather than focusing on what customers are doing in their buying process.

Too many sales processes employed by companies are, in essence, a checklist of activities that the seller associates with moving a customer toward a sale. Proper sales strategies use an assessment to execute each step through the sales pipeline to determine where the customer is in the process of making a buying decision. Too often sellers operate as though activities such as completing a SWOT analysis, having a first meeting or submitting a proposal constitute a sales strategy. While each of these steps is important to making a sale, they are only half the story. What's missing is the perspective of the customer.

Effective pipeline progression relies on incorporating the customer's point of view and continually realigning the steps in the sales process accordingly. Without the customer's point of view woven throughout a company's sales process, there is a danger of opportunities being worked based on salespeople's assumptions and guesses as to where an opportunity is in the pipeline and what is required to progress it to close. Understanding the distinction between the seller's point of view and the customer's point of view is critical to producing accurate pipelines.

If, for example, you are attending an important customer meeting in another state, it is likely that a salesperson may need to buy a plane ticket, drive to the airport, park his or her car, fly to the city where the meeting is being held, catch a taxi to the customer's location, register at the front desk, and so on. While each of these activities is critical to the salesperson's attendance, they have little direct impact on the quality of the meeting, to say nothing about whether or not this is an opportunity that eventually will close.

Consider the kinds of milestones that are built into most sales pipelines. Huthwaite's research indicates that sales pipelines often reflect the sales equivalent of these kinds of activities. Is it any wonder that pipeline milestones such as "initial meeting completed" and "delivered capabilities presentation" contribute to bloated pipelines and inaccurate forecasts?

Incorporating the customer's perspective in the pipeline means answering such questions as

- "Has the customer revealed explicit needs that this solution will address?"
- "Has the customer described the decision-making process he or she will use for this specific opportunity, including buyer roles?"
- "Has the customer provided access to senior-level decision makers?"

- "Has the customer revealed how this initiative will be funded?"
- "Has the customer discussed his or her decision criteria and ranking of their importance?"
- "Has the customer shared his or her perceptions of risk in moving ahead with your solution?"

These are examples of questions that, if built into the pipeline process, will provide the essential qualifying steps needed to weed out the deals that will drive up sales costs and decrease revenues.

By applying greater rigor to understanding the quality of opportunities in the pipeline, not just the quantity, a far more realistic sales funnel emerges. The *real funnel* differs from the feel-good funnel in that it

- Has fewer opportunities in the earlier stages
- Has less projected revenue in the pipeline

These are two revelations that make sales managers extremely nervous. The notion of having less activity, opportunities, and dollars in the pipeline goes against every traditionally held sales paradigm.

On deeper scrutiny, however, the real funnel has a much higher percentage of deals that have a greater likelihood of closing. This has several implications:

- Salespeople can focus their time and energies on better-qualified opportunities.
- Managers can focus their coaching efforts on opportunities that have a higher likelihood of rewarding their efforts.
- Forecasting will become more objective, accurate, and rewarding.
- Sales costs will decrease significantly.
- Profitability per salesperson, per client, and per organization will climb.

The real funnel eliminates time, money, and effort expended on hopeless causes. It uses a process that qualifies out those deals that have little likelihood of closing, and salespeople are instead focusing their time on opportunities that are winnable. They are forecasting opportunities that have a significantly lower risk of disappearing from the pipeline. Not only does the pipeline focus on the opportunities that have a real potential to close, but it also increases the velocity of those opportunities because they are properly qualified in the early stages.

Managers are directing their coaching efforts in ways that make a real difference to revenue. As with eating too much ice cream, just because something feels good does not always mean that it is the right thing to do. Sales managers draw tremendous satisfaction from seeing a sales pipeline that surpasses revenue targets at each stage. The feelings of achievement and anticipation that this brings can obscure the gray reality that these pipelines are sometimes being viewed through rose-colored glasses. By applying qualitative milestones at the early stages of the pipeline and equipping salespeople with the necessary skills to execute on those milestones, companies can quickly weed out the distractions and see dramatic improvements in their sales force's focus, energy, success, and revenues.

As Attila's horde lost focus on the winnable big battle—which they could have won had they maintained discipline at Orleans—so too salespeople can lose focus on the winnable big deal. Getting caught up in the many robs the few of the right attention. *Auri sacra fames.*

# 26

## THE SIEGE OF HARA CASTLE
## THE SHIMABARA REBELLION (1638)

### THE SILENT KILLERS

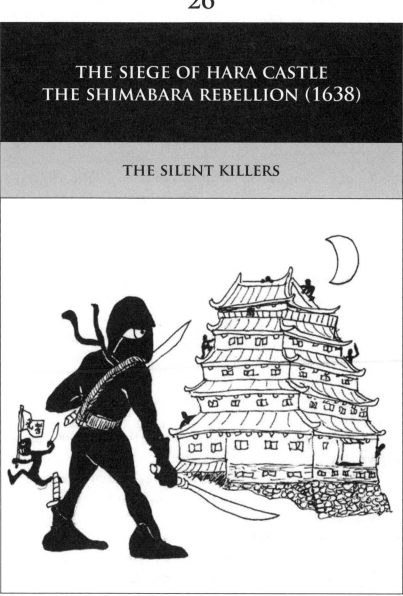

*Secret operations are essential in war; upon them
the army relies to make its every move.*
—SUN TZU

In the autumn of 1637, Christian peasants in the Shimabara Peninsula and the Amakusa Islands of Japan rose in revolt against the horrible cruelty and tyranny of the local *daimyo*, Lord Matsukura Shigemasa. All local attempts to end the uprising failed. The rebellion eventually attracted the attention of the Tokugawa Shogunate at Edo, which sent an army to quell the unrest. More than 30,000 rebels, with a force of mercenary *ronin* (masterless Samurai), holed up in the dilapidated Hara Castle and held out for several months before their final defeat in April of 1638.

One of the contributing factors to the undoing of the resistance at Hara Castle was the use of Ninja for espionage and subversion. Ninja tactics during the siege provide the sales lesson from the Shimabara Rebellion: *Beware the silent killers.*

**WHAT HAPPENED** Life was hard for poor tenant farmers in seventeenth-century Japan. By 1637, in Shimabara and the Amakusa Islands it had become untenable. Persecution of Christians in this largely Christian area was rampant and brutal. And economic conditions were unbearable. Oppressive taxes, awful collection methods, and forced labor were the order of the day. Peasants who could not pay their taxes were treated awfully.

In October 1637, at last having reached their limit, the peasants rose up against their tormentors. Under the charismatic leadership of 16-year-old Amakusa Shiro, armed with farm implements, rocks, and a fair number of Samurai swords in the hands of roving *ronin*, the rebels attacked the town of Shimabara in the southern part of Kyushu Island some 750 miles south of Japan's capital at Edo. They rid themselves of the local magistrate and set the town ablaze.

This raised eyebrows throughout the district. Lord Terazawa Katakata made preparations for the defense of Nagasaki and then dispatched 3,000 Samurai from northern Kyushu to put down the rebellion. The little force of Samurai failed, and the attempt at pacification failed.

The rebel army soon swelled to some 35,000—not counting many women and children. They took possession of an abandoned castle at the southern tip of the peninsula known as Hara Castle. With massive walls and three moats, they reckoned themselves safe there. The whole rebellion was now under one roof. They had chosen the Christian cross as their banner, giving the thing a bit of a religious flavor.

On January 4, 1638, a small group of Ninja from Koga in central Japan arrived at the castle and began surveillance and espionage operations that lasted two weeks. They secretly entered the castle every night, collecting intelligence on the defenses, provisions, and so on. One mission apparently included a provisions theft, depriving the castle of much-needed food stores. The Ninja sent a very detailed report to the Shogun.

In a matter of just a few weeks, Tokugawa Iemitsu, Shogun at Edo, had responded by putting together a force of nearly 150,000 troops to besiege Hara Castle. The siege lasted for three months. On April 15, 1638, the Siege of Hara came to an end. The rebels—who were at last hungry and exhausted—finally capitulated. The government was utterly merciless in victory. *Caedite eos. Novit enim Dominus qui sunt eius.*

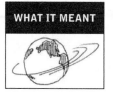

**WHAT IT MEANT**

The Shimabara Rebellion marked the end of Japanese foreign relations for more than two centuries. It was the final excuse the Shogunate needed to expel all foreigners from the islands. Japan went into isolation and was closed to foreign visitors until the arrival in 1853 of U.S. Navy Commodore Matthew Perry, who reopened trade with Japan at the Convention of Kanagawa the following year.

The Tokugawa Shogunate entered a period of unchallenged power for nearly 250 years—one of the longest periods of unbroken peace in the history of the world. This also was the last time that Ninja were used in battle.

**SALES LESSON**

The sales lesson we derive from the Shimabara Rebellion stems from the legendary character and behavior of the Ninja warrior. It is the danger of the silent killers: the hidden costs of sales.

Popular corporate thinking says that to increase profits, all a company needs to do is increase sales revenue.

Unfortunately, much of this profitable growth is compromised by the hidden costs that business leaders do not see.

The typical categories that organizations list on the cost-of-sales side of a revenue spreadsheet include such things as travel costs; commissions; the total compensation of people working on the bid divided by the number of customer meetings, calls, and internal planning meetings; external consultants; printing and materials costs; telecommunications; and marketing.

The reason these costs are listed is because they are obvious.

But there are costs that are not so obvious. These insidious costs are usually overlooked and do not appear in profit calculations. Nevertheless, these hidden costs have just as critical an impact on profitability per deal, per salesperson, per region, per client, and ultimately, per company.

If you had to guess which destroys more homes every year in the United States, which would you choose—fires, floods, hurricanes, or earthquakes? The answer is none of the above. According to the insurance industry, there is another destructive force that destroys more homes every year than all these combined. Termites. These vicious little critters are quietly destroying homes from the inside out. Such are the internal costs of sales, quietly eating away at your bottom line. These termites of the corporate world are to be found in the unconscious behavior of your salespeople and managers during a typical sales cycle.

One of the major causes of escalating sales costs is the misalignment of what organizations measure and what actually contributes to sales success. If you ask a sales leader how he or she measures success of a salesperson, the ultimate answer is revenue. This can be dressed up in any number of ways, such as quota achievement, stronger customer relationships, territory coverage, lead-to-conversion ratio, and other such terms. But make no mistake, the purpose of all these is to drive revenue.

There are several quantitative measures that sales leaders typically use as leading indicators for pipeline management:

1. *Dollar amount in the pipeline* (e.g., "We need to have a total pipeline value of $4.3 million if we are going to hit our team target")

2. *Number of opportunities in each stage of the pipeline* (e.g., "The success profile in our company is eight opportunities in stage one, five in stage two, four in stage three, etc.")
3. *Sales activity* (e.g., "Our salespeople need to see five customers and have six telephone sales calls per week")

These are the quantitative measures that many sales leaders will say form the foundation for how they run their business. However, sales leaders who laud their pipeline management ability also will quietly mention that they are facing such challenges as

- Sales reps chasing business they have little chance of closing
- Sales reps not redirecting their efforts to focus on better opportunities
- Managers coaching opportunities that never progress
- Managers coaching salespeople who never seem to get better
- Stalled pipeline opportunities
- Deal slippage from month to month
- Inaccurate forecasting

Huthwaite's position is that the quantitative measures used so frequently by leaders to predict future revenue, while important, provide an incomplete and frankly incorrect view of the true accuracy of your pipeline and the sales costs your sales teams are unconsciously creating. These quantitative measures must be balanced with qualitative measures if the challenges mentioned earlier are to be prevented. By applying qualitative measures to your leading indicators, you will realize that

1. It is not the dollar amount in your pipeline that matters—it is the dollars associated with opportunities that are being worked on and are progressing.
2. It is not the number of opportunities in your pipeline that matters—it is the number of opportunities that have a realistic chance of closing.

3. It is not how many sales calls your salespeople have that matters—
   it is how many sales calls that end with a customer commitment
   that moves the opportunity forward.

I have identified five critical qualitative measures. I call them the
*silent killers* because, like termites, they typically go unseen.

## SILENT KILLER 1: MISALIGNMENT OF SALES ACTIVITY AND REPORTING WITH THE PHASES OF THE CUSTOMER DECISION CYCLE

The kinds of commitments that buyers make and the areas of focus that
they adopt change dramatically as they move from stage to stage of the
buying cycle described in Chapter 14. Buyers in recognition of needs,
for example, focus on defining a problem or an opportunity in terms of
what a successful outcome or solution will look like. Buyers in evaluation of options are focused on differentiating between the various suppliers vying for their business. They form decision criteria and use those
criteria as a lens through which to examine the capabilities and offerings
of each potential supplier. In resolution of concerns, buyers are evalu-
ating the consequences of following through on a tentative decision.
After the buying decision is made, buyers in the implementation phase
are looking to measure their actual success against the vision of success
created earlier in the decision cycle. Finally, buyers in changes over time
do not yet recognize a need for change and typically are comfortable
with the status quo.

A customer's perception of value will vary depending on what phase
of the buying cycle he or she is in at any given time. Therefore, the
selling skills that deliver that value also need to vary depending on what
phase of the buying cycle the customer is in.

Developing an effective sales strategy requires the seller to have
three skills:

1. The ability to recognize where the buyer is in the decision cycle
   at any particular time

2. The ability to execute the specific skills that create value for the customer at each phase

3. The ability to move a buyer both forward and backward in the decision cycle

These are the skills required to execute a strategy. Misalignment of sales approach with what the customer values in each phase is a leading cause of deal stagnation—those opportunities that initially promise so much but seem to go nowhere and eventually are removed from the pipeline after months of scrutiny.

## SILENT KILLER 2: FAILURE TO CAPTURE EXPLICIT NEEDS DURING CRITICAL EARLY-STAGE SALES CALLS

Many salespeople fall into the trap of assuming that just because a customer states a problem that the salesperson's offering can solve, that constitutes a pipeline opportunity. The key skill is to elicit an explicit need from the customer (see Chapter 4). Doing so has been revealed by Huthwaite research to almost double the likelihood of success of a sales call. If salespeople are pursuing and forecasting opportunities based only on implied needs, then they are dangerously overestimating the value of those opportunities.

## SILENT KILLER 3: SELLING TO THE WRONG BUYER

Many salespeople claim that their strength as a seller lies in their ability to build good customer relationships. Because of this skill, they are able to get appointments seemingly at will, and their customers speak very highly of the positive relationship with them. They even seem to be very skilled at finding new opportunities on a regular basis. But too often a deeper dive into a relationship builder's pipeline opportunities reveals a consistent theme—the relationships are being built with people in the customer organizations who do not have any significant spending authority. There are three distinct buying influences in every major sale, each with its own needs, and each requiring a different selling approach. You cannot sell the same way to all of them and expect positive outcomes.

## SILENT KILLER 4: ACCEPTING CONTINUATIONS FROM CLIENTS

The distinction between an advance and a continuation (see Chapter 11) is critical for the health of your pipeline. Opportunities that are built on sales calls that conclude with advances are deals that deserve time and attention. Resource these opportunities. Opportunities that are built on sales calls that conclude with more continuations than advances are a drain on company resources. The most successful sellers are the ones who are able to consistently achieve advances. Salespeople pursuing opportunities and forecasting revenues based on nice-sounding continuations are a leading contributor to missed forecasts and unnecessarily high sales costs.

## SILENT KILLER 5: MANAGERS FOCUSING THEIR COACHING EFFORTS ONLY ON LATE-STAGE OPPORTUNITIES

Huthwaite conducted a revealing study in a large multinational organization to see if there is any correlation between when in the sales cycle a manager gets involved and sales-cycle length. The researchers discovered that if managers were active in the sale during the critical early sales calls, this had a direct impact on the length and, by default, cost of those sales. If the ability to create maximum value for clients lies in the recognition of needs phase of the buying cycle, managers need to be focusing some of their time on helping their people execute this phase more effectively. It is in this phase that they can have the most impact on customer issues and customers' perceptions of the size of their problem, size of the solution, and ultimately, the perceived value of your solution to the customer.

Eliminating the silent killers starts with answering two important questions:

1. Can you incorporate milestones that measure the quality as well as the quantity of opportunities in your pipeline?
2. Do your salespeople and managers have the necessary skills to execute these pipeline milestones?

Pipeline data based only on quantitative measures combined with salespeople's opinions on deal progression and likelihood of closing allow the termites of the corporate world to munch happily away at the foundation of an organization.

# 27

# NAPOLEON'S MARCH ON MOSCOW
# THE GRAND ARMY VERSUS
# THE RUSSIANS (1812)

## ON THE IMPORTANCE OF GOOD FORECASTING

*If you can look into the seeds of time, and say which*
*grain will grow and which will not, speak then unto me.*
—WILLIAM SHAKESPEARE

Napoleon began his invasion of Russia with the largest army ever gathered in the annals of war up to that time. It consisted of nearly half a million Frenchmen, Prussians, and Austrians. Ten thousand men survived. Napoleon had made certain assumptions regarding his overwhelming force. First, he incorrectly believed that the Russians would fight a pitched battle rather than resorting to a scorched-earth policy. Second, he assumed that his supply lines would hold up and that he could forage along the way—also negated by Tsar Alexander's scorched-earth policy. Third, he assumed that the weather would hold and that he would be victorious and home before winter. Unfortunately for him, winter arrived early and extraordinarily harsh in 1812. The combination of bad assumptions destroyed Napoleon's army and his power in Europe. *Libenter homines id quod volunt credunt.*

Historians derive a wide variety of lessons from this famous disaster, usually relating to hubris. The lesson I shall derive is on the *importance of rational forecasting.*

**WHAT HAPPENED**

Napoleon's Russian Campaign in 1812 may have been one of the greatest blunders in military history. The Grand Army entered Russia from Poland with a force of 422,000. Of those, 100,000 made it to Moscow. Ten thousand made it home.

Napoleon's motives for the campaign seem to have been twofold: (1) to force Russian Tsar Alexander's participation in the European trade embargo against the British and (2) ostensibly to protect Poland against a possible Russian invasion.

The Grand Army crossed into Russia in mid-June 1812 and began its epic trek toward Moscow. Some argue that Napoleon was lured ever deeper into the vast and unforgiving wilderness that was Russia in the early nineteenth century by the purposeful policy of nonengagement practiced by the Russian commanders Field Marshal Barclay de Tolly, Peter Bagration, and the old veteran, Prince Mikhail Kutuzov. The Russians just kept retreating, and Napoleon just kept following them.

After several minor engagements—most notably at Smolensk—the armies finally met on the field of battle at Borodino on September 7.

It was a clash of empires. While technically a victory for Napoleon, it was certainly Pyrrhic because his soldiers were irreplaceable owing to logistics. The Russian Army managed to retreat toward Moscow, most unwisely followed by a vastly weakened Grand Army. Napoleon still hoped that he could destroy the Russians at Moscow. But the Russians passed through Moscow without stopping—except to evacuate the city and then set it on fire.

Napoleon arrived in Moscow a week after the great battle in time to watch it burn to the ground. He entered a city that was left empty of food for his men or forage for the horses. Napoleon now made a fatal blunder. For reasons never fully explained—but apparently waiting in vain for a Russian surrender—Napoleon remained with his army in Moscow until October 20. This bizarre decision accomplished nothing except to absolutely guarantee a disastrous retreat from Moscow. The Grand Army, now in tatters, faced a terrible march home through lands that had already been plundered and scorched, without hope of supply. And, of course, this was during the miserable Russian winter that came early that year. In addition, the Grand Army was hounded by Cossack raiders and a reinvigorated Russian Army, which caught up and nearly destroyed them at the crossing of the River Berezina.

After the crossing, the army had utterly fallen part. Napoleon himself fled the scene—deserting his army for the second time in his career (the first was in Egypt in 1799). Riding hard, he was back in Paris in four days, pretending nothing was amiss. Meanwhile, there was nothing left of the once proud and formidable Grand Army but a hopeless mob trying desperately to survive. The whole affair was an unmitigated and almost unimaginable disaster.

**WHAT IT MEANT**

France's failed Russian Campaign of 1812 was the beginning of the end of the Napoleonic Wars. The Russian victory proved once and for all that Napoleon was not in fact invincible—indeed, that while certainly a military genius, he was fallible in the extreme. It marked a turning point in European history.

The campaign has been memorialized in such epic masterpieces as Tolstoy's *War and Peace* and Tchaikovsky's *1812 Overture*.

Napoleon's failure to engage in rational forecasting (of the weather, for one thing; of Tsar Alexander's intentions, for another) is highlighted by his decision to stay in Moscow for five weeks. It was a fatal blunder. Sales leaders have much to learn from this mistake.

Sales executives typically describe forecasting with one of two statements:

> "The only way I come close is by making my own gut-feel alterations to the exaggerations of my salespeople."

> "There has to be a better way of generating numbers."

Accurately forecasting sales numbers is the bane of most sales executives' existence. While everyone accepts that effective management requires accurate information and metrics, few sales executives are satisfied with the sales-forecasting tools or processes they employ. Most rely on the perceptions of their salespeople about which business will close and when. Unfortunately, this approach leaves the manager exposed to the vagaries of subjectivity because each salesperson either hedges or exaggerates. Under these circumstances, sales forecasting is more alchemy than science.

But there is hope. Inaccurate forecasts are unnecessary, and they do not result simply as a failure of process. Inaccurate sales forecasting is a symptom of a more pernicious problem—failing to incorporate the customer's point of view in the development and implementation of sales strategy. If the seller and the selling organization craft sales strategies on the basis of buyer behavior, creating a forecasting model of exceptional accuracy is relatively straightforward. In fact, the skills and tactics of customer-focused selling are the basis of good forecasting.

Let's discuss two central conclusions:

- *Poor forecasting is only the symptom.* The real problem is sales strategy that lacks customer-centricity in both focus and execution.
- *Effective forecasting tools and processes do not need to be complicated or overly analytical.* They are the natural product of good strategic planning.

In an ideal world, salespeople and their managers would be able to predict future sales results with a high degree of accuracy, at least for the period of one future sales cycle. This should hold true regardless of the length of the sales cycle.

While it may be difficult to predict each individual piece of business (particularly with new opportunities in early sales pipeline stages), forecasting sales numbers in the aggregate should be nearly as reliable as the forecasts most businesses make of "controllable" operations such as their manufacturing processes. Sales management should be able to apply the same concepts of variance reduction (such as Six Sigma) to sales forecasts that other managers use to control nonsales processes.

This is more than a matter of just giving comfort to company leaders. Wall Street punishes the smallest negative variance in profit predictions. A half a percent shortfall in earnings can cause stock prices to plummet. For companies that are less concerned with public equity markets, consider the impact that unpredictable revenue figures can have on budgeting, financing, and discretionary spending.

Good forecasting requires a set of leading indicators that give salespeople and sales managers an easy-to-use tool for predicting the likelihood of revenue from each individual account and opportunity. However, these kinds of metrics are rarely developed and used. Much more common are seat-of-the-pants predictions by overly optimistic or consistently conservative salespeople, modified according to equally subjective judgments by sales managers.

If such leading indicators are to be identified, the starting point is a proven sales strategy that is executed according to what the customer is doing at any given moment to reach a buying decision. For the sake of this discussion, let's assume that *sales strategy* refers to the steps salespeople take in either closing a new opportunity or deciding that the business cannot be won.

It is important to point out that this assumption is a fairly significant one. Many companies allow their sales force to develop new opportunities with little more than an ad hoc this-is-the-way-we-have-always-done-it approach. When done properly, sales strategy, like all other parts of the sales function, is a matter of science, not folklore. One point cannot be overstated: It is impossible to move forecasting beyond pure guesswork unless the sales force has a common set of practices for developing customer-centric sales plans.

Be careful not to confuse sales strategy with a simple checklist of activities that the seller associates with moving a client toward a sale. Real sales strategies use an assessment of where the customer is in the process of making a buying decision to adjust and execute each step through the sales pipeline. Too often sellers operate as though activities such as completing a SWOT (Strengths, Weaknesses, Opportunities, Threats) analysis or submitting a proposal constitutes a sales strategy. While each of these steps is important, and in some cases is essential, to making a sale, they represent steps in only one-half the process. What's missing is the perspective of the customer.

Real strategy relies on incorporating the customer's point of view and continually realigning the steps in the sales process accordingly. Why is the customer's point of view so important? Imagine the parent whose only attention to childrearing was a checklist of activities to be completed as the child reached particular ages and who was oblivious to how the child reacted or developed. No one would call this good parenting. Yet many sellers look at activities such as completing a SWOT analysis as their only method of planning competitive positioning. Isn't the customer the final arbiter of who wins the business? How does the seller know that his or her own SWOT analysis coincides with the customer's view?

Well-formulated and well-executed sales strategies incorporate both a seller and a buyer focus. Good strategies juxtapose insights such as those gained through SWOT analysis with considerations such as customer buying criteria and how the customer ranks the seller against these criteria. By comparing these two points of view, the seller can identify strengths and weaknesses in the sales strategy. These strengths and weaknesses are the basis for adjusting the strategy and tactics of seeking a customer's business.

This means that sound strategies are dynamic. When done properly, the seller adjusts the plan with every new piece of information obtained.

It is the ability to plan and execute such strategies that forms the basis for great forecasting. Let's dissect this idea by looking at the tool most people use in place of a strategic plan—the sales pipeline.

Too often sales pipelines are constructed with milestones that register activity rather than events. Effective strategies are those which focus on events and on customer commitments, not just on checking off which activities a salesperson has completed. It is a mistake to depend on pipeline milestones such as "customer gap analysis defined," "initial sales meeting completed," "customer audit performed," or "proposal submitted." These so-called milestones have little to do with measuring the effectiveness of a sales strategy and even less to do with how to measure the likelihood of closing a sale. Yet it is just these kinds of measures from which forecasts are so often constructed. No general would enter a battle and determine strategy based on such things as "guns loaded" or "marching orders issued." These activities are not inconsequential, but they contain no valuable data as to where the battle plan stands with regard to its objectives.

Great sales strategies and pipelines that track sales progress measure events rather than activities. This distinction is critical to producing accurate forecasts. If, for example, I am attending an important client meeting, it is very likely that I need to buy a plane ticket, drive to the airport, park my car, check in at the hotel in the city where the meeting is being held, and so on.

While each of these activities is critical to my attendance, they have little direct impact on the quality of the meeting. Reflect, however, on the kinds of milestones that are built into most sales pipelines. Do they reflect the sales equivalent of these kinds of activities? Huthwaite's research indicates that they often do. Is it any wonder that pipeline milestones such as "submitted a proposal" or "delivered capabilities presentation" contribute to poor forecasts?

In short, effective sales strategies require planning that identifies the outcomes of events as the basis for moving toward a sale. The primary distinction here is that *events* incorporate the customer's point of view, whereas *activities* have a seller-only perspective. Therefore, if strategy is the linking of events to achieve a specific sales outcome, then it is these kinds of events that should constitute the milestones in the pipeline tool we use to forecast.

If the pipeline tool has been developed with these ideas in mind, then accurate forecasts are the natural outcome of using the tool. Effective pipeline tools therefore are representations of two aspects of each sale: the events that the seller has conducted or completed arrayed against the buyer's incremental commitments to make a buying decision. Let's take a look at how these things work together.

I begin by establishing a set of discrete steps in the sales process that track each opportunity as it moves from "suspect" to "contract." It matters little whether this cycle is represented as having three stages or 30. What is necessary is that each stage legitimately represents some significant change in the orientation of the strategic seller. What drives movement through the pipeline are the commitments and actions taken by the buyer as he or she moves closer to making a buying decision.

Few sales forces seem to have the ability to execute sales strategies based on customer buying behavior. Although many companies might disagree, their lack of accurate forecasting is prima facie evidence of this conclusion. Many companies have implemented elaborate CRM systems with high hopes of improving sales forecasts. To some extent, these expectations do materialize. Collecting a wealth of data where no such data existed before obviously will add some science to a previously subjective methodology. But these improvements only mask the underlying problem. In truth, accurate forecasting is the natural bedfellow of the ability to execute a customer-driven strategy. And a customer-driven sales strategy is the key to a short, effective, and high-percentage sales cycle.

# 28

## PYRRHUS OF EPIRUS CAMPAIGN AGAINST THE ROMANS (280–279 BC)

### ON THE PYRRHIC VICTORY (OR NOT BUYING REVENUE)

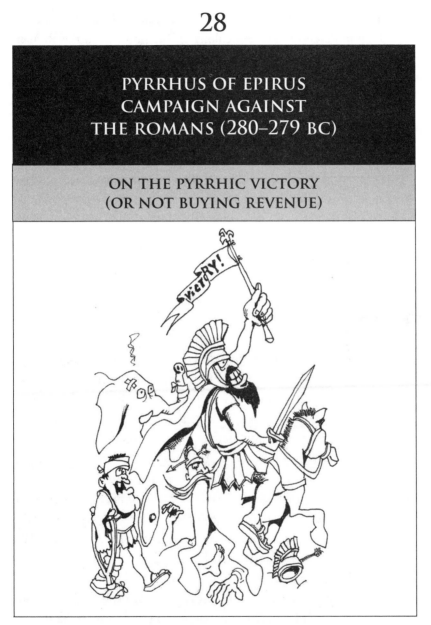

*Look upon my works, ye mighty, and despair.*
—PERCY SHELLEY, OZYMANDIAS

K ing Pyrrhus of Epirus, the famous Greek general, was called to Italy to defend the Greek colony of Tarentum from the Romans in 280 BC. He arrived with a great army, including the Epirot cavalry and fighting elephants. He defeated the Romans at Heraclea in 280 BC and then again at Asculum in 279 BC. After news of the second victory arrived, however, Pyrrhus' response was, "One more victory like this and we shall be undone." He has given his name to the Pyrrhic, or too expensive, victory. *Flet victus, victor interiit.*

In the world of sales, a too costly victory is that huge account that costs more to acquire than it's worth. It may be that it's not profitable, or it may be that it sucks up resources ad infinitum. Regardless, it is a piece of business you couldn't afford to win and now can't afford to keep, or it will sink you.

**WHAT HAPPENED** Tarentum, a Greek colony in southeastern Italy, was at war with the Romans, who were campaigning to conquer and unite all Italy. The Tarentines had exhausted their resources, and a good deal of demagoguery and blathering had prevented them from coming to terms (thank goodness our politicians today don't act like that!). In the end, they decided to ask King Pyrrhus of Epirus to be their general. Pyrrhus was not only the most skillful commander (Hannibal regarded him as the greatest of all generals) but also happened to be the one man of his caliber in Greece who actually would welcome the adventure. Pyrrhus agreed and arrived in Italy with his Epirot army. He first sought peace by arbitration and mediation but was rejected by the Romans. Pyrrhus advanced to the River Siris and encamped in the plain between the cities of Pandosia and Heraclea.

When the Romans tried to cross the river, Pyrrhus led his men into battle, charging at the head of his cavalry. He was splendid (and conspicuous—which I'm not sure is necessarily a good thing in battle, but there we are) in his rich and beautiful armor. And he led the whole army, moving back and forth between infantry and cavalry, masterfully directing the battle. After being felled from his horse, however, and safely whisked from the field by a small group of friends, he exchanged armor with his friend Megacles. Megacles was soon afterwards set on and killed by a couple of enterprising Romans. The Romans raised Megacles' head on a spear and brandished it before their troops, claiming to have killed Pyrrhus.

The Romans were naturally delighted and starting cheering. The Greeks were dismayed in equal measure and became disheartened. Pyrrhus, perceiving what had happened, stripped Megacles' helmet from his head and rode about the place showing his bare face to his army. It was enough. The Epirots attacked with a renewed vim and vigor, and the Greek elephants ran amok among the Romans, in the end causing complete disarray. Pyrrhus ordered the Thessalian cavalry to charge, which it did. The Romans were scattered. They had lost the day. But Pyrrhus had lost "the flower of his men, and amongst them his particular friends as well as officers whom he most trusted and made use of" (Plutarch, *Lives of Illustrious Men*, "Pyrrhus").

Pyrrhus advanced to within 37 miles of Rome itself, collecting confederate cities along the way. The Romans, for their part, were not ready to quit. They had a steady stream of replacements and reinforcements and continued to refuse talk of peace, but rather they continued to threaten war and more war. Pyrrhus, after resting his men, prepared for a second fight. The battle came near the city of Asculum. On the first day of battle, the terrain was wooded, pretty much useless for cavalry, and a swift river prevented the elephants from joining the infantry. Night put an end to the day's fighting.

On the second day of the battle, Pyrrhus left a detachment in the woods and brought the main army of slingers, archers, and elephants into the open field. Pitched battle ensued on plain ground. Pyrrhus himself—wounded in the arm by a javelin while fighting most courageously—and the elephants are credited with finally breaking the Roman lines. "The armies separated; and, it is said, Pyrrhus replied to one that gave him joy of his victory, that one other such would utterly undo him. For he had lost a great part of the forces he brought with him, and almost all his particular friends and principal commanders;

there were no others there to make recruits, and he found the confederates in Italy backward" (Plutarch, *Lives of Illustrious Men*, "Pyrrhus"). Plutarch reckons that more than 15,000 men died in the battle.

**WHAT IT MEANT**

King Pyrrhus has lent his name to the too-expensive victory:

**Pyrrhic victory**—a devastatingly costly victory or a goal achieved at too great a cost; a victory that is offset by staggering losses.

Pyrrhus fought his final battle with the Romans at Beneventum in 275 BC. After retreating from the battlefield, he decided it was time to go home. His defensive campaign on behalf of the Tarentines was losing steam, and he was running out of allies, so he returned to Greece with the remnant of his army. According to Plutarch, his parting words were, "What a battlefield I am leaving for Carthage and Rome." Most prescient, if true.

By 270 BC, Rome had conquered the last Greek colony in Italy (Rhegium) and was now master of the Italian peninsula. Rome had begun its ascendancy in the Mediterranean.

**SALES LESSON**

As can happen on a battlefield, so can it happen in business. The cost of sales can be too great to sustain growth in a company; it can bleed a company to death. For Pyrrhus, the cost of the campaign to protect the Greeks in Italy cost him many of his friends, his best generals, and too many irreplaceable elite Epirot veterans.

Let's look for a moment at a consummate example of the Pyrrhic victory in business. Rubbermaid is one of the best known brands in America. The company makes all manner of things plastic; one or another of its 5,000 household products is in virtually every home in America. In February 1994, Rubbermaid was chosen "America's Most Admired Company" by *Fortune* magazine. It was described as "master of the mundane and a champion innovator." In 1999, Rubbermaid sold out—in a fire sale—to Newell, one of its major competitors. How could this happen? Interestingly, it all began with a genuine Pyrrhic victory by Rubbermaid.

Former Rubbermaid CEO Stanley Gault, who served through the 1980s and early 1990s, bet the farm on supplying big-box discount chain stores. He claims to have read the proverbial tea leaves and discovered that the future was not thousands of customers but rather a few massive customers. Walmart was the Holy Grail. Walmart was Gault's single-minded quest—and he achieved it; he at last sold his wares to Walmart. And Walmart became his largest customer by far. At this point, the ghost of Pyrrhus may well have been hovering at his shoulder wondering at what cost would this victory come.

At first, the arrangement was extremely advantageous; it fueled Rubbermaid's meteoric rise in the early 1990s. Just a few months after being unabashedly admired by *Fortune*, however, Rubbermaid found itself in deep waters. The price of resin went through the roof in the spring of 1994. In fact, it doubled. And resin is a vital raw material in almost all of Rubbermaid's products—which raised manufacturing costs significantly. To survive, Rubbermaid simply had to raise its prices. When the company broke the news to Walmart, the world's largest and most powerful company simply said that it would not accept a price increase. Period. Even though the proposed increase was less than a double-digit percentage, Walmart flatly refused and dropped a number of Rubbermaid products from its inventory. The blow all but destroyed Rubbermaid.

Over the next few years, the loss of its largest account, coupled with relatively lax management, sent Rubbermaid spiraling downward. It would never recover, and in 1999, Rubbermaid was sold to Newell for $5.8 billion (most of which was merely for the brand name). Assets were auctioned off, and the company was no more. Last year Walmart was number nine on *Fortune's* "World's Most Admired Companies" list.

Rubbermaid's massive reliance on one huge and powerful account turned out to be a major strategic error. In the end, it destroyed the company. But this is not uncommon in sales. Too often even veteran salespeople make the mistake of placing their bets on the one huge account that will, in theory, sustain them. But it doesn't.

And there are other types of Pyrrhic victories in sales—which, unlike the quintessential example of Rubbermaid, happen every day. They may not be as dramatic—indeed, they are often quiet and insidious—but they are just as destructive.

Many factors play into hollow victories in sales. Some are related to the cost of sales, which continues rising dramatically. Others have to do with underestimating the expectations of customers, who tie up more resources than the selling company anticipated after the sale. And finally, there are those internal factors that, when understood, can be controlled.

The economic downturn has had a notable and, many say, irreversible effect on the rigor that organizations and individuals put into purchasing. Budgetary restraints have placed a higher degree of oversight on decision making. This often lengthens the sales cycle by extending the resolution of concerns phase of the customer buying cycle—owing to high levels of perceived risk and uncertainty. Add to this the explosive growth of competition in all industries, with many new offshore competitors willing to undercut on price in order to establish a foothold in new markets, and you have a whole new breed of buyer that is causing an escalation in the price of selling.

Moreover, customers can treat sellers as commodities because they have many more options for any particular solution. Prospects have begun acting like customers long before they sign a contract. They want more meetings, demonstrations, proofs of concept, access to experts, and so many other requests once reserved for paying customers. And they can—because if one selling organization won't play by their rules, another will. This is one of the major reasons why the cost of pursuing opportunities has skyrocketed and continues to climb and why sellers need to be so much more strategic in deciding which opportunities to pursue. For some organizations, opportunity selection has rightly become a Six Sigma process.

Customer expectations and demands from selling organizations also can be rather extreme—paying customers, that is. The aforementioned demand for meetings, demonstrations, proofs of concept, access to experts, and so forth uses up time and money that is rarely compared directly with the revenue generated by the account. It is chalked up as the cost of doing business. Comparing the cost of doing business with revenue generated in particular cases may reveal Pyrrhic victories in almost any organization.

One of the main internal causes of escalating sales costs is the misalignment of what organizations measure and what actually contributes to sales success. If you ask a sales leader how he or she measures success of a salesperson, the ultimate answer is revenue. This can be dressed up in any number of ways, such as quota achievement, stronger customer relationships, territory coverage, lead-to-conversion ratio, and other such terms. But make no mistake, the purpose of all these is to drive revenue.

Revenue as a success metric is a lagging indicator. It is a backward-looking metric because by the time you can measure it, it is too late to affect it. So organizations have established a series of forward-looking metrics, or *leading indicators*, that provide a determination of whether or not an individual or organization will achieve revenue targets in the future.

Unfortunately, most leading indicators are quantitative measures that have only some relation to sales success. In every company I poll, these measures always fall into one or more of three categories (as I noted in Chapter 26):

1. *Dollar amount in the pipeline* (e.g., "There needs to be a total pipeline value of $4.3 million in order to hit the team target")
2. *Number of opportunities in each stage of the pipeline* (e.g., "The success profile in the company is eight opportunities in stage one, five in stage two, four in stage three, etc."
3. *Sales activity* (e.g., "The salespeople need to see five customers and have six telephone sales calls per week")

These quantitative measures so frequently used by leaders to predict future revenue, while important, provide an incomplete and frankly incorrect view of the true accuracy of a pipeline and the sales costs that sales teams are unconsciously incurring. Quantitative measures must be balanced with *qualitative* measures if the real cost of sales is to be seen. As noted in Chapter 26, by applying qualitative measures to leading indicators, one discovers that

1. It is not the dollar amount in the pipeline that matters—*it is the dollars associated with opportunities that are being worked on and are progressing.*
2. It is not the number of opportunities in the pipeline that matters—*it is the number of opportunities that have a realistic chance of closing.*
3. It is not how many sales calls a salesperson has that matters—*it is how many sales calls that end with a customer commitment that moves the opportunity forward.*

Pyrrhic victories in sales are commonplace—much more commonplace than is usually imagined. There are the dramatic cases such as Rubbermaid, but then there are the many cases in which revenue—a good thing—is devoured by the cost of sales or, more often and less visibly, the cost of doing business. Pyrrhus shuddered at the news of his "victory." Sales leaders no doubt would shudder more often than they do if they recognized the actual costs of sales and just doing business in relation to the revenue generated. Pyrrhus left the battlefield open to Rome and Carthage and Rubbermaid to Newell.

# 29

## BATTLE OF GRAVELINES
## THE BRITISH ROYAL NAVY VERSUS THE
## SPANISH ARMADA (1588)

### ON BALANCING EFFICIENCY AND EFFECTIVENESS

*Efficiency is doing things right; effectiveness is doing the right things.*
—PETER DRUCKER

The small village of Gravelines, near Calais, France, saw the decisive battle of the Spanish Armada against the British Navy. The British ships were better armed and more maneuverable, so the British commanders decided to change the rules of naval warfare. Prior to that time, guns were used to support ramming and grappling. The British decided to use them to destroy Spanish gun crews and sink Spanish ships by keeping up an unrelenting cannonade. Adopting this strategy, the British were able to keep their distance and prevent boarding by superior Spanish marines. It worked. The British finally backed off when they ran out of ammunition, but they had caused enough devastation to set the Spaniards to flight. Of course, much of the Armada was then destroyed by gales off Scotland and Ireland in the North Sea.

The lesson that I draw from the British Navy at Gravelines is as follows: It is in fact possible to balance efficiency and effectiveness, and to do so is ever so important to the success of a sales manager.

**WHAT HAPPENED**   In 1588, King Philip II (aka "Philip the Prudent") of Spain took the not-so-prudent step of trying to invade England and depose Queen Elizabeth I. The relationship between the two sovereigns was complex in the extreme. Spain and England had a historic alliance—centered in large part on their mutual fear and hatred of France. In fact, Philip was married to Elizabeth's half-sister Mary I and actually was King of England while Mary I reigned. When it became clear that Philip and Mary would have no heir, Elizabeth's future succession to the throne appeared to be certain. The following year, in 1556, Philip became King of Spain and began a policy of protecting Elizabeth. *Bella gerant alii, tu felix Austria, nube.*

In 1558, Elizabeth was crowned Queen of England, and Philip helped her to consolidate her power over the next decade. Then it all fell apart. This was so in part because the French threat had collapsed in the face of religious and civil strife. Elizabeth and Philip eventually came to hate each other—not least over the question of religion. Elizabeth established the Protestant church, which became the Church of England, whereas Philip threw himself heart and soul into the Catholic Counter-Reformation. Their disagreement became intensely personal.

Mary Stuart, the deposed queen of Scotland, arrived in England in 1568 with a claim to the English throne. As a devout Roman Catholic, she was supported by Pope Pius V—who excommunicated Elizabeth in 1570. Philip also thought Mary Stuart a good alternative, despite her French connections. In 1571, he was implicated in the infamous "Ridolfi plot" to assassinate the Queen. Elizabeth never forgave him this impudence.

In the early 1570s, England began building a formidable navy on the advice of John Hawkins. The new ships were faster, more maneuverable, and had more and better guns than their Spanish counterparts. In 1580, Elizabeth knighted Francis Drake—who had brought her treasure from a Spanish galleon he had captured off Peru while circumnavigating the globe in the *Golden Hinde*. In allowing this, Elizabeth had, for all practical purposes, broken the tenuous peace.

Philip began preparing an armada for an invasion of England. After a number of setbacks, a plan was set in motion for the Spanish Armada (transporting 18,000 Spanish soldiers) to rendezvous with Alexander Farnese, Prince of Parma, and his Army of Flanders (26,000 crack troops) at Dunkirk and from there to invade Kent.

On July 29, 1588, the Spanish Armada—consisting of 127 ships—arrived within sight of England. The English fleet, under the command of Baron Howard of Effingham, Lord High Admiral, sailed out with around 160 ships. The first cannonades were fired on the morning of July 31, but the decisive battle did not happen until over a week later.

On the morning of August 8, English galleons attacked the Spanish off the coast of Flanders near Gravelines. The Spanish Armada was massively outgunned, and the wind and current favored the English. The ensuing Battle of Gravelines lasted for nine hours. It was decisive.

The battle began with Drake's *Revenge* trading broadsides from somewhere between 50 and 100 yards with the Spanish flagship *San Martin*. British light guns on the upper decks wreaked tremendous damage on the enemy's rigging and sails and caused havoc among the marines who lined the rails. Meanwhile, the heavier guns on the lower decks did tremendous damage to the hull. Such was to be the new rules of naval warfare. The old paradigm in which ships served basically as platforms for hand-to-hand fighting at sea was abandoned completely.

The British Navy kept its ships just out of reach of Spanish boarding parties but kept up an unrelenting fire from close quarters. In the end, the British won the day; the Spanish Armada retreated. The new British brand of fighting at sea had proven both efficient and effective.

**WHAT HAPPENED**

The Spanish Armada was a spectacular failure. Most of the damage and casualties actually came after the Battle of Gravelines. The Armada was forced by the winds into the North Sea, where it was severely punished by gales off Scotland and Ireland.

Philip was humiliated. He tried to send more armadas over the next several years, but all attempts failed. Elizabeth, for her part, may not have been the great hero she pretended. As it turned out, she was unable to pay the nearly 12,000 sailors and troops who had saved her kingdom.

**WHAT IT MEANT**

The importance of balancing efficiency and effectiveness emerges as the great lesson from the Battle of Gravelines. It has been said of efficiency and effectiveness that these two metrics are often mutually exclusive or at least natural enemies: You can either get it fast or get it right, but you can rarely get both at the same time. Often, it seems, you can have one or the other but not both (unless you are lucky or you want to spend a lot of money). Indeed, it is a rare and delightful occasion when the two work in concert. The good news is that the skeptics are wrong. In coaching, you can in fact balance the two—and derive the most benefit from both. But it is sometimes a delicate (which is not to say precarious) balance.

Efficiency metrics are activity measures, whereas effectiveness metrics are outcome measures. Efficiency measures productivity; effectiveness measures quality. The key word for our purposes is *balance:* There is a balance that must be struck between efficiency and effectiveness. Fortunately, it does not take very much effectiveness measure to counterweight an enormous amount of efficiency measure. Effectiveness measures tend to be leading indicators (because they are indicative of something about the client), whereas efficiency measures tend to be lagging indicators—if that.

Efficiency is a measure of activity: number of calls, opportunities in the pipeline, total value in the pipeline, forecast values, and so on. These numbers are important; they are the metrics we use to manage a business. In fact, the higher up you go in an organization, the more you will find these numbers relied on for decision making because they are the pure and objective data by which business decisions are made.

Effectiveness has degrees of achievement versus degrees of economies: Did you pique their interest? Did you meet any of their desires or needs? Did you get a callback? Did you get a sale? Did you maintain a relationship or account?

Efficiency relates to the economical application of resources. Effectiveness relates to the success of the application in achievement of objectives. The problem with measuring only efficiency indicators is that *what is measured is what gets done*. When the focus is on measuring activity, activity will be done in spades, for its own sake. In tough times, managers have a tendency to push harder on the accelerator of efficiency, which is to say that they push for more activity—and they get all the activity they want. But it doesn't go anywhere. And they get into a death spiral where the more they demand, the more they get, and the fewer outcomes they get from it. And down they go.

The other problem with efficiency measures is that they tend to be very defeating to top performers because top performers are focused on outcomes, not activities. It is the average performers who focus on activities. So average managers tend to chase off top performers from their companies at the very time when they are needed most. The truth is, as the research shows, more does not equal better in consultative sales, and in fact, it may be counterproductive because onerous paperwork and fruitless racing about generally frustrate top performers. In major sales, success comes from working *smarter*, not *harder*.

Sales efficiency is about how to get in front of customers for the right amount of time at a minimum cost. Sales effectiveness is about how to maximize sales potential once you're there. The methods that increase efficiency are very different from the ones that increase effectiveness.

Many sales organizations have run into severe troubles because they have tried to apply efficiency solutions to effectiveness problems and vice versa. Many major sales managers damage their own success and the success of their people by intentionally adopting *selling-harder* solutions for *selling-smarter* problems.

Great sales managers find the balance—optimal efficiency metrics and practical effectiveness measures. Recall that just a few effectiveness measures will balance a myriad of efficiency measures. Efficiency metrics are quantitative; effectiveness measures are done in ratio form, for example, did a call plan lead to the desired outcome? In essence, effectiveness metrics are oriented to a ratio measure of whether or not a progressive outcome resulted from an individual activity. Efficiency can be improved by activity management and territory configuration, for example. Effectiveness improvement requires training, modeling, and great coaching. Great coaches help their salespeople to understand the importance of outcomes.

The prerequisite for striking a balance between efficiency and effectiveness is the ability to understand customer behavior. Customer behavior is the only indicator of effectiveness. The only indicator that we have done a good job is that the customer has said, "I'm willing to act"—whether that's to make a purchase or to make an interim step. If the customer is not reacting, our activity is going nowhere. And if all we are measuring are activities, we have no idea what the client or customer is doing. The good news is that it only takes two or three effectiveness measures to counterweight all the activity. If we had just a few ways of understanding how the customer behavior maps to what we are doing, the world would come up roses. Few sellers know how to read or how to elicit customer behavior, so they are lost in a sea of activity. Great coaches help to sort this out by putting in place a few effectiveness measures.

The single most important function of a manager in consultative sales is to improve the effectiveness of salespeople. Nothing else a sales manager does, whether it's brilliant selling, superlative administration, canny politics, or outstanding negotiation, has one-half the potential impact that comes from doing a good job of building sales effectiveness.

Sales effectiveness isn't the easiest concept to grasp, although there are rich rewards for those who can do so. On the surface, effectiveness can be defined simply as those things a salesperson does during the sales cycle that cause the customer to decide in the salesperson's favor. Unfortunately, such a broad definition doesn't help managers to grapple with the practical issues of how to improve effectiveness. You can't help salespeople to be more effective unless you have a clear idea of what effectiveness looks like. Some managers are able to recognize effective selling when they see it, but only a small fraction is able to describe the component behaviors. It's not easy to identify those specific behaviors, but it *is* important. By having a clear and detailed picture of what effective sales behaviors look like, you can diagnose effectiveness problems in your people, and through coaching, you can improve their skills significantly. Your understanding of effective behavior translates directly into sales productivity.

The great thing in managing consultative selling is to balance efficiency metrics with effectiveness measures. The balance can be struck— and just a little effectiveness provides a great counterweight to a large amount of efficiency—but the balance is fragile. Do not be tempted to spend undue time on activity measures because they are easier to quantify. Real and lasting improvement in your sales force depends on great coaching, and great coaching focuses on effective sales behaviors. Learn the effective selling behaviors, and coach to them relentlessly. The research is conclusive: It will pay handsome dividends.

# LATIN QUOTES

CHAPTER 1
*Amat victoria curam.* "Victory loves preparation."

CHAPTER 2
*Gladiator in arena consilium capit.* "The gladiator is making his plan in the arena [i.e., too late]" (Seneca).

CHAPTER 3
*E mare libertas.* "From the sea, freedom."

CHAPTER 4
*Unus homo nobis cunctando restituit rem.* "One man, by delaying, restored the state to us" (Ennius).

CHAPTER 5
*Concordia salus.* "Well-being through harmony."

CHAPTER 6
*Ab obice saevior ibit.* "The resistance only makes him attack more ferociously."

CHAPTER 7
*Aut nunc, aut numquam.* "Now or never."

CHAPTER 8
*Virtus, non copia vincint.* "Courage, not multitude, wins."

CHAPTER 9
*Bona diagnosis, bona curatio.* "Good diagnosis, good cure."

CHAPTER 10
*Aequam memento rebus in arduis servare mentem.* "In difficult situations, remember to keep your mind clear."

CHAPTER 11
*Aut vincere, aut mori.* "Either conquer or die."

CHAPTER 12
*Deserta faciunt et pacem appellant.* "They create a desolation and they call it peace" (Tacitus).

CHAPTER 13
*Cura omnia potest.* "Determination is omnipotent."

CHAPTER 14
*Difficile est tenere quae acceperis nisi exerceas.* "It is difficult to retain what you may have learned unless you should practice it" (Pliny the Younger).

CHAPTER 15
*Cuiusvis hominis est errare.* "Every human can make a mistake" (Cicero).

CHAPTER 16
*Alea jacta est.* "The die is cast" (Caesar).
*Trahimur omnes laudis studio.* "We are all led by our eagerness for praise" (Cicero).

CHAPTER 17
*Audaces fortuna iuvat.* "Fortune favors the brave" (Virgil).

CHAPTER 18
*Caveat aemuli.* "Beware the competitors."

CHAPTER 19
*In magnis voluisse sat est.* "In big things, it's enough to just have the will."

CHAPTER 20
*Audere est facere.* "To dare is to do."

CHAPTER 21
*Aliam vitam, alio mores.* "Another life, other values" or "Other times, other manners."

CHAPTER 22
*Alta alatis patent.* "The sky is open to those who have wings."

CHAPTER 23
*Clara pacta, boni amici.* "Clear agreements, good friends."

CHAPTER 24
*Non omnes qui habent citharam sunt citharoedi.* "Not all those who own a musical instrument are musicians" (Varro).

CHAPTER 25
*Auri sacra fames.* "The cursed hunger for gold."

CHAPTER 26
*Caedite eos. Novit enim Dominus qui sunt eius.* "Kill them all. The Lord will know His own" or "Let God sort them out."

CHAPTER 27
*Libenter homines id quod volunt credunt.* "Men gladly believe that which they wish for" (Caesar).

CHAPTER 28
*Flet victus, victor interiit.* "The conquered moans, the conqueror is undone."

CHAPTER 29
*Bella gerant alii, tu felix Austria, nube.* "Others may lead wars, you, happy Austria, marry."

# INDEX

# ABOUT THE AUTHOR

**John Golden** joined Huthwaite as president and CEO in August 2008. John's track record as a proven leader combined with extensive experience in the learning industry provides the foundation for his strategic vision of success for Huthwaite. Since joining he has been responsible for successfully rebranding the organization as well as redefining its value proposition and go-to-market strategy. He has also introduced new and innovative technology-

Photo by Jonathan Thorpe.

enabled tools and capabilities to complement core offerings.

Prior to his work with Huthwaite, John served as the senior vice president of Education and Business Development at the Mortgage Bankers Association. Golden joined MBA from Learning Sciences International, a startup company providing professional development products for K–12 educators, where he was vice president of the educational services division and responsible for defining and executing the go-to-market strategy. Before that, Golden was vice president of products and programs and a member of the senior executive team at New

Horizons CLC, the world's largest independent IT training company, where he managed a $32 million business unit responsible for sourcing, building, and providing products and services to franchise locations in more than 50 countries.

Golden started his career in the learning industry at SmartForce (formerly CBT Systems) in Dublin, Ireland before moving to the corporate HQ in Silicon Valley, California where he was responsible for developing and bringing to market key strategic initiatives including the launch of the first fully integrated online learning platform. John received his undergraduate degree from Trinity College in Dublin, Ireland and his Master of Arts from Dublin City University, also in Dublin, Ireland.